JACQUES MERCIER

THE
TEMPTATION
OF CHOCOLATE

ÉDITIONS
Racine

The story of chocolate

Dear Readers,

Chocolate, with its secular history, the beneficial effects we derive from eating it, the vast variety of items available in top quality gastronomic products, the aura of luxury brands and its conquest of the entire world are all thrilling and fascinating.

Until now, no book had been written about how the history of chocolate crossed paths with the fascinating tale of the international, yet clearly Belgian, adventure of the inventor of the chocolate that the Belgians happily call the 'praline', and its legendary style of packaging: the 'ballotin'.

We therefore asked Jacques Mercier (a well known Belgian author and media personality) to write the story of two legendary tales which have intertwined through the ages: the evolution of chocolate, originally a ritual beverage of the Aztecs – the cocoa bean also being used as their currency – and the history of the Belgian praline which has conquered the most refined gourmet palates throughout the world.

Jacques Mercier is one of the most well informed experts on the world of chocolate and its history. For the preparation of this book, he carried out considerable in-depth research which led to the discovery of several stories and anecdotes about this wondrous product that had not been published previously.

The result is a history book which, far from being austere, is the story of the evolution of chocolate through the ages and throughout the world, intertwined with the history of the legendary Neuhaus brand. The original Neuhaus shop, dating back to 1857 which was the cradle of the brand, still exists today in one of the oldest glass-covered streets in the world: the Galeries de la Reine in Brussels.

We are delighted, dear Readers, to invite you to enjoy reading this saga as much as we have enjoyed it.

Guy Paquot
Chairman, Neuhaus

Jos Linkens
CEO, Neuhaus

1
The invention of the praline

2
The Discovery of Chocolate

3
The Chocolate Route

4
Belgian chocolate

5
Chocolate's place in History

6
The transformation of chocolate

7
Chocolate Production

8
Chocolate varieties

9
The Art of Chocolate

10
The flavours of Neuhaus chocolate

11
Some chocolate recipes

Do not resist temptation!

"The temptation of chocolate" is a reference to the legendary Neuhaus pralines: *Tentation* and *Caprice*. They are triangular in shape, lovingly created by hand – wonderful craftsmanship – and are made of nougatine filled with a coffee-flavoured ganache or vanilla fresh cream. *Tentation* has a milk chocolate coating and *Caprice* has a dark chocolate coating. There is a film behind the origin of how these names were chosen. The anecdote is that Pierre De Gavre, a descendant of the Neuhaus family, who had the idea of using these two names after hearing them in the dialogue of a film in 1958. They were pronounced with bewitching sensuality by a film star who fascinated him at that time: a certain Brigitte Bardot!

Chocolate is the food of the gods, just as the elixir of youth that kept Cleopatra young through its *aloe vera* vitamins, and it is akin to nectar, the honey beverage, and to ambrosia that was the food of the gods of Mount Olympus that gave them their immortality. Chocolate is a mythical food and a mythical beverage! It is also the name given by Carl von Linné to the cocoa tree in the 18th century: *Theobroma Cacao L.* from the Greek meaning "food of the gods". The origins of chocolate, the legends and history – the broad historical outlines concerning its discovery, the chocolate route and its transformations, and the anecdotes and miscellaneous tales – all contribute to the sublimation of chocolate!

Moreover, chocolate features in our memory, even without realising it, in association with the happy and carefree times of childhood celebrations, birthday parties and chocolate flavoured treats enjoyed in the school playground; every time we taste chocolate, we feel happy.

→ *Theobroma Cacao,* 18th century. Natural History Museum, London.

The term 'passion' is also associated with chocolate. It describes not only those of us who appreciate chocolate in all its forms, and those of us who love food; it also describes the creators of chocolate. They are true artists, passionate about their profession. Not unlike alchemists, they transform raw material, in this case the cocoa bean, into an exquisite food or a delicious drink. Just like a painter who takes a dab of colour from his palette and creates a stunning work of art, or a poet who knows how to choose the right words that come together and form a magnificent verse!

Chocolate, reminiscent of wine, has its own vocabulary, similar to that used by wine experts. A chocolate can be rich, light, sweet, fruity, etc.

Our senses are truly tempted by the variety of pralines that exist. How can we resist when, after having tasted the first praline in the box, we suspect that the dainty mouthful alongside it may contain a filling so delicate that we are already imagining the taste of the chocolate coating on the tongue and how it would taste as it glides down the back of the throat! "Happy chocolate, which having circled the globe through women's smiles, finds its death at their lips." (Brillat-Savarin)

How can we resist when we know that tasting chocolate activates our five senses! Firstly, we see the look of the chocolate: matt, shiny, ivory, satin-like, or dark brown. Then we touch it before putting it in our mouth, the chocolate can feel rough or smooth; we take the first bite and the sound delights our ears; the chocolate coating melts on the tongue and the four primary flavours – sweet, sour, salty and bitter – meld together. It is smooth and creamy. When the filling appears beneath the slightly melting outer chocolate shell, it is through the retronasal route that the aromas of vanilla, coffee, praliné and gianduja (almond and hazelnut flavoured) are inhaled.

The stimulation of the five senses takes us to seventh heaven! How can we possibly resist chocolate?

Oscar Wilde wrote a great deal about temptation: "I can resist anything but temptation"[1], "The only way to get rid of a temptation is to yield to it"[2], and about caprice: "The only difference that exists between a caprice and a life-long romance is that a caprice lasts a little longer"![3]

Jacques Mercier

1 *Lady Windermere's fan.*
2 *The picture of Dorian Gray.*
3 *Essays.*

CACAO. Off.
Theobroma Cacao. *Bot.*
Der Cacao.

The invention of the praline

Jean Neuhaus settles in Brussels

In the year 1857, the spring and summer seasons were very hot and there was talk of the end of a "short ice period". In Paris, Baron Hausmann started major transformation works in the French capital. The poet Alfred de Musset died. The founder of the scout movement, Robert Baden-Powell, was born. While, in Switzerland, Frederic William IV of Prussia renounced his role as suzerain over the canton of Neuchâtel, the Swiss citizen and resident of Neuchâtel, Jean Neuhaus decided to settle in Brussels. Together with his brother-in-law, a pharmacist, he opened a pharmacy-confectioners boutique at 25-27 Galerie de la Reine. Close to the Grand-Place, the "Passage Saint-Hubert", as it was called, was a 200-metre long gallery, covered with a glass roof. The press called it "the world's most luminous passage". The first King of the Belgians, Leopold I laid the foundation stone in the presence of the Dutch architect Jean-Pierre Cluysenaer.

← Neuhaus Boutique, Galerie de la Reine, Brussels.

↓ Jean Neuhaus, who founded Neuhaus in 1857.

The passage took its name from the "Saint-Hubert" tavern which had a shop sign featuring the saint; the tavern was very popular with the stall-holders from the nearby Marché aux Herbes *(herb market)*, Rue Saint-Hubert linked the market to the famous Rue des Bouchers. In the shop, Jean Neuhaus sold large quantities of cough sweets, marshmallows, and liquorice to cure stomach ache. The area enjoyed a huge success. The Galerie de la Reine became a much frequented and fashionable address, and also a choice meeting place for cultural activities. For example: the Café de la Renaissance, which nowadays is the "Taverne du Passage" was the meeting place of the Arts and Literature Circle, which boasted illustrious writers and poets as its members, including Baudelaire, Alexandre Dumas, Victor Hugo, Apollinaire and Verlaine.

After the death of his brother-in-law and associate, Jean Neuhaus asked his son Frédéric Neuhaus (1846-1912) to join him in Brussels. The younger Neuhaus started studying the profession of Master Confectioner so that he would be qualified to follow in his father's footsteps in due course. They preferred Belgium to Switzerland,

Frédéric Neuhaus, son of
the founder Jean Neuhaus.

Jean Neuhaus, who took over
the business in 1912.

despite the fact that the chocolate business was becoming rapidly established in Switzerland.

As early as 1792, the Josty brothers opened a chocolate boutique in Berne, followed by a shop in Berlin at the beginning of the 19th century, selling "excellent chocolates" according to reports written at the time. In 1819, François-Louis Caillier inaugurated the first Swiss chocolate factory in Corsier, near Vevey. In 1826, it was the turn of Philippe Suchard to go from having a boutique in Neuchâtel, where Jean Neuhaus could well have been a client, to inaugurating a chocolate factory in Serrières. Several years later, he opened a warehouse in Paris. In 1830, it was the turn of another legendary name in the history of chocolate to found his chocolate factory: Charles-Amédée Kohler, who invented chocolate containing hazel nuts. Jean Tobler then followed in 1868, Rudolph Lindt in 1879, Alexis Séchaud in 1884 and so forth...

One anecdote among many recalls that the Russian poet Alexander Pushkin, several hours before his death in 1837 in a duel with his wife's alleged lover, had a chocolate drink at the Chinese Café in St. Petersburg, prepared by two Swiss, who owned the café and who came originally from the Grisons region: Salomon Wolf et Tobias Béranger!

In Switzerland, the Neuhaus name is still alive, mostly due to Charles Neuhaus (1796-1849) who was a tradesman and a leading political figure. There is a foundation and museum built in honour of his memory in Bienne, in the canton of Berne, established in the building of a former factory, called Verdan-Neuhaus, producing "Indiennes", painted or printed cotton textiles. The site was bequeathed to the foundation by its last owner, Dora Neuhaus (1889-1975). The origin of the family name goes back to their forbears who originated in northern Italy. When they came to Switzerland, their name was "Casanova" (new house) and then they changed it to "Neuhaus" to make it sound more Swiss.

In Brussels, things developed gradually in Galerie de la Reine, next to the medicinal sweets, the Neuhaus boutique offered caramel sweets, jellied fruits and vanilla

flavoured chocolate. Business developed so well that in 1895, Jean Neuhaus and his son Frédéric founded the Neuhaus-Perrin Confectionery and Chocolate factory. This was a period of great success for chocolate in Europe and in Belgium in particular: in 1905, there were some fifty chocolate factories and by 1913, eight years later, there were 150!

Frédéric Neuhaus died in 1912 and his son Jean Neuhaus (1877-1953), took over the company. The decor of the boutique, situated at n° 25-27 created in 1912 remained unchanged right up to the end of the 20th century. However, 1912 was also a historic year for another reason; it was the year of the creation of the praline.

↑ Neuhaus Boutique, Galerie de la Reine, *circa* 1915.

DESSINS ET MODÈLES INDUSTRIELS

PROCÈS-VERBAL DE DÉPOT

Aujourd'hui, le _seize_ du mois d' _Avril_
mil neuf cent et _quinze_ à _deux_ heures et _demie_ de l'après-midi,
(heure belge), trois heures vingt-six minutes, (heure de l'Europe
centrale), Monsieur Jean Neuhaus, confiseur, demeu-
rant à Bruxelles, Galerie de la Reine 25,

se présente au greffe du Conseil de Prud'hommes de la ville de Bruxelles et y dépose
une enveloppe cachetée qu'il dit contenir (b) _l'échantillon d'un modèle_
industriel (enveloppe en carton pour bonbons),
dont il veut se réserver l'usage exclusif (c) _à perpétuité_ ;
le quel (d) _modèle_ Mr _Jean Neuhaus prequalifié_
déclare se rapporter à (e) _l'industrie du cartonnage et à celle_
de la confiserie et du chocolat et de tous autres pro-
duits alimentaires

LE DÉPOSANT,   LE GREFFIER,

Jean Neuhaus   Verolme

N° 3432

The creation of the praline and the 'ballotin'

In 1912, Jean Neuhaus (Junior) created a chocolate that he named "praline"; this was to become one of the best known and most appreciated of Belgian creations worldwide. The possible origin of the term "praline" goes back to a certain Marshal du Plessis-Praslin whose cook, curiously named Lassagne, discovered a sweet by pure chance when browning grilled almonds in the remains of some boiling sugar. He noticed one of his kitchen boys nibbling a piece of melted sugar! Monsieur de Choiseul, Duke of Plessis-Praslin (1598-1675) was the ambassador of the French King Louis XIII and it was during the siege of Bordeaux when the people rebelled against the authority of the King that the incident took place. The word was written as "prasline" in the beginning, then as "praline" from 1680 onwards. After having won many glorious honours, the Marshal retired to Montargis. There he founded the "Maison de la praline", which exists to this day.

However, another explanation of the term seems just as plausible. The verb "praliner" in French, ("to puddle" in English) is an agricultural term meaning coating the roots of a plant or the seeds with fertilizer before placing them in the earth, and also the act of coating them before putting them inside for winter storage. In both cases, there is a parallel with the filling and coating of the chocolate. There must surely have been an exchange of influences. The praline was registered in 1912 and its success was immediate.

The most obvious way of selling pralines, in Belgium that is, was to pile them up like chips or other food in a paper cornet. However, the pralines got scratched and

← The registration document for the 'ballotin' registered by Neuhaus in 1915. Register of industrial designs and models, La Fonderie, Brussels.

↓ Some of the oldest pralines: Bonbon 13 (1937), Astrid (1937), Manon sucre vanille and Manon sucre café (1937), Caprice (1958) and Tentation (1958).

Ballotin 1929

Ballotin 1915

Ballotin 1975

Ballotin 2003

Ballotin 1985

Top right, the Neuhaus
ballotin, design registered in
1915 at Council of Industrial
Relations in Brussels.
La Fonderie, dépôt agr,
industrial designs and
models, Council of Industrial
Relations, Brussels.

Ballotin 1980

Iron box Tintin 1993

spoiled, and the ones at the bottom of the cornet were crushed. Louise Agostini (Jean Neuhaus's wife) discovered a way of presenting the pralines without damaging them: she invented the "ballotin", the chocolate box made of cardboard. The pralines were placed inside the box, side by side in separate layers. The registration document for the design is dated 16 August 1915, at 2.30 p.m. (Belgian time) and at 3.26 p.m. Central European time! The text reads, "Mr Jean Neuhaus, confectioner, residing in Brussels, Galerie de la Reine, 25, appeared before the clerk of the Council of the Industrial Relations Tribunal in the town of Brussels and presented a sealed envelope which he declared contained a sample of an industrial model (a cardboard container for chocolates), whose use he wishes to reserve for himself exclusively in perpetuity; Mr Jean Neuhaus declared that the said model is peculiar to the cardboard industry, the confectionery, chocolate and all other food industries". The name of the clerk was H. De Boelpape. This 'ballotin' was so practical that all Jean Neuhaus's colleagues asked him to grant them the right to use a similar cardboard box for their companies' products (which meant that they did not have to pay royalties!). They all met regularly at the Royal Association of Master Confectioners of Belgium, which held an exhibition just before the war in the Madeleine ballroom, under the patronage of HM Queen Elisabeth, with the participation of England, France and the Netherlands. Jean Neuhaus generously allowed them to do so, preferring their friendship to the fortune that he could have earned. His daughter Suzanne Neuhaus told me "My parents invented the 'ballotin', in order not to damage the pralines. It replaced what was not actually called the cornet but rather the pouch. Yes, my father was adorable, and he did not take advantage of the possibility of earning royalties."

↑ Suzanne De Gavre-Neuhaus
in the role of Manon Lescaut
in 1942, composed by
Jules Massenet, La Monnaie
Theatre Archives, Brussels.

→ Horace Vernet,
The cocoa seller, 19th century.
Private Collection.

Louise Agostini, the inventor of the 'ballotin', inherited her artistic talents from her great-grandfather who was a sculptor. She suggested that Neuhaus should have a unique style and had the idea of using the N of Napoleon and decorating the boutiques and 'ballotin' in the imperial colours of green and gold. This style marked generations of chocolate lovers in Belgium and all over the world. As from 1918, the famous Galerie de la Reine boutique hosted many famous visitors: the Prince of Wales and the young Belgian Prince Leopold visited the boutique to make their purchases in person. The success was so enormous that the Neuhaus workshops were transferred to 23-27 rue Van Lindt, in Anderlecht.

In 1923, Jean Neuhaus's son-in-law took over the business. Jean Neuhaus's daughter Suzanne had married Adelson De Gavre, and it was he who created the famous pralines *Tentation* and *Caprice* (names chosen by their son), which are still included in the current range of Neuhaus pralines. Suzanne De Gavre-Neuhaus also inherited artistic talents from her mother and her mother's family. She is an opera singer, soprano and mezzo-soprano, and is a highly appreciated performer at the Belgian opera house, Théâtre de la Monnaie. She has played leading roles in *The Barber of Seville*, *La Bohême*, *La Traviata*, *La fille de Madame Angot*, and especially Manon Lescaut in *Manon*, composed by Jules Massenet – which is why the Manon praline is so popular! Moreover, she asked the costumier of the prestigious opera house, James Thiriar, to renew the Neuhaus decorations, packaging and designs. She told us, "When I was an opera singer, I gave artistic advice about the business and also asked friends to help. Thus, the Monnaie's famous decorator designed a special chocolate box featuring characters from *La fille de Madame Angot*." He designed the "Friendship Packages" for the chocolate boxes sent to the Congo, when the Congo was a Belgian colony. Belgians living in the Congo even opened chocolate boutiques. "We could not use fresh cream in the fillings for the Friendship Packages," she added, "We used nougat. Each praline was wrapped in silver paper and placed in a presentation box... until the arrival of expanded polystyrene, flights took less time and there were refrigerated warehouses."

La Marchande de Coco.

Dessiné par C.e Vernet.   Gravé par Debucourt.

The only difference that exists between
a caprice and a life-long romance is that
a caprice lasts a little longer"

(Oscar Wilde)

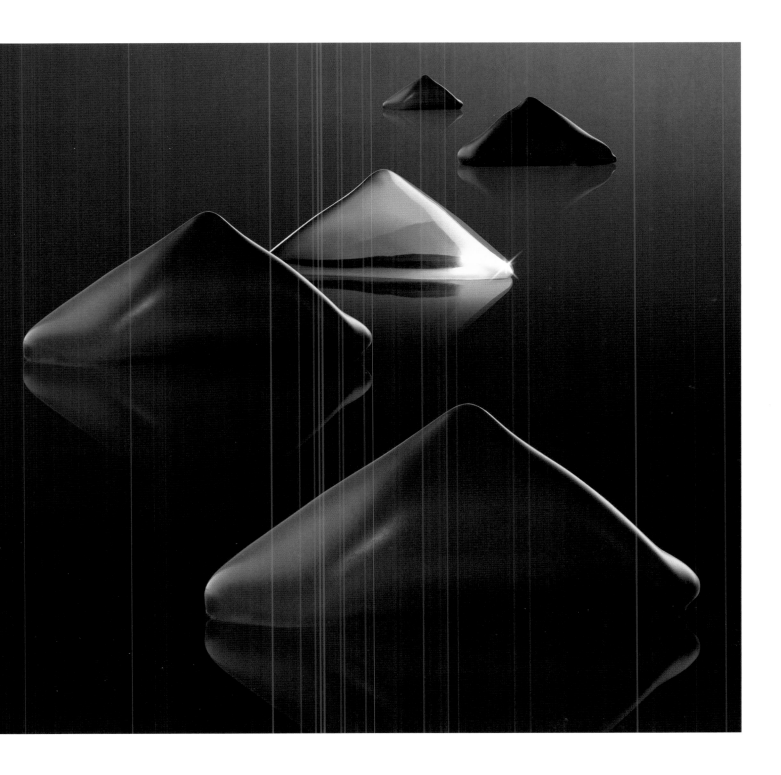

Neuhaus expands in Belgium

→ Jean Neuhaus, third on the left, in front of a grinding machine.

The first boutique opened after the Second World War was in Le Zoute. Suzanne Neuhaus remembers it well, "Immediately after the Liberation, we decided to open a Neuhaus boutique in Le Zoute. The day of the inauguration, we had to cross Place Albert on a wooden gangway, because there was still a large anti-tank ditch there! Baroness Vaxelaire said to my mother, 'A boutique in Le Zoute, such madness! They will certainly need ten years to rebuild everything!' But a year and a half later, everything was finished. When I went with my father to visit the site where the boutique was going to open, we went via Damme. Along the canal, on the left side, there were German corpses and on the right side Canadian corpses. Prisoners of war were digging them up to put them in body bags and bury them in military cemeteries. Le Zoute was liberated five or six months after Brussels. The Germans had stayed there well armed to ensure a passage to the Netherlands and the launching ramps for the V1 rockets..."

The son of Suzanne Neuhaus and Adelson De Gavre, Pierre, was very young when he learned the secrets of chocolate making. (It was he who thought of the names *Tentation* and *Caprice*). He looked, listened, and helped. His father was quick to share the management role with him. It is Pierre who invented franchising. "We were the precursors of franchising", he said. "People involved in sales came to do a six-month internship at Galerie de la Reine; we called them "satellites". Of course, they had to sell our products, but not solely our products: we asked them to be attentive concerning the decoration, trinkets and chocolate boxes and to follow the fashion according to the time of the year. It was therefore a form of franchising before franchising had been invented".

Jean Neuhaus, as all master chocolate makers, was always very concerned about the quality of raw materials; he even pushed perfectionism to the point of visiting Venezuela to negotiate the exclusivity of the cocoa bean production. He was received by President Gomez, known as "the man with sixty women". The negotiations were arduous, but finally, the contract was signed by the Venezuelan President on the condition that a picture of the Venezuelan flag feature on certain packaging with the mention "special plantation selections", in addition to a picture of the President!

→ Next page:
Pierre De Gavre on the far left in the praline workshop.

↓ Offices and praline packaging workshop in 1948.

The 1970s, the years of expansion

At the beginning of the 1970s, Adelson De Gavre became President of the Association of Confectioners and Chocolate Makers of Belgium. Neuhaus was acquired by the Ceuppens group and Pierre De Gavre left his position as head of the company. In 1974, the De Beukelaer company acquired Neuhaus. In 1978, the brothers Jean-Jacques and Claude Poncelet, already involved with the Mondose and Verhaeren chocolate makers, took over the Neuhaus business and, at the same time, they acquired Corné Port-Royal. This step marked the internationalisation of the Neuhaus firm. 'Pralineries' were launched in the United States in Dallas, Los Angeles and Charleston. Luxury department stores sold Neuhaus products in Canada, Columbia, Guadeloupe and Japan.

In 1987, the sugar refinery Raffinerie Tirlemontoise acquired Neuhaus, when it celebrated its 130th anniversary. At that time, the company was worth BEF 300 million and was producing 800 tonnes of pralines. In 2005, Neuhaus was Number One with 2,900 tonnes of product exported to 48 countries. The company's head office and its production centre were transferred to Sint-Pieters-Leeuw (Vlezenbeek) in Flemish Brabant. Neuhaus's American subsidiary, Neuhaus Inc USA established its offices at Fairchild Avenue, 120, Plainview, 11803 New York.

In 1987, Neuhaus acquired a 66% stake in the "Jeff de Bruges" brand. This company was founded in 1986 by Philippe Jambon, who still heads up the firm. "Jeff" is the first name of Jeff Verheecke, a chocolate maker from Bruges who originally made the chocolates. Today, the company is the market leader in France; there are some 250 stores bearing the "Jeff" name and 220 of them are in France.

From 1987 to 1991, Jacques Barbé was the managing director of Neuhaus. Between 1991 and 2003, there was a woman managing director leading the company, Marlène Vonken. Neuhaus was introduced on the stock exchange in February 1997 by the Artal group, which withdrew as a shareholder in March 1999. The Compagnie du Bois Sauvage then became the leading shareholder in Neuhaus. In 2000, on the occasion of Dynasty Day, His Majesty, King Albert II granted Neuhaus the title of Accredited Supplier to the Belgian Court. Since 2003, Jos Linkens has been

Neuhaus, accredited supplier to the Belgian Court since 2000.

KING POWER INTERNATIONAL CO. LTD
8 RANGNAM ROAD PHAYA THAI
KWEANG THANON PHAYA THAI
KATCHAO BANGKOK
THAILAND
TH-10400
PO 224100
PO 224100

FIN

NEUHAUS CASABLANCA
BOULEVARD ZERKTOUNI 192
MA-CASABLANCA
MOROCCO
TEL +00212
FAX 07-05/07
FAX 07-05/0

DUFRY SINGAPO
#038-036 PAS
CHANGI AIRP
SG-SINGAPORE
SINGAPORE
PCH2007050
PCH2

USA

RECEIVING BANK FOR KCC
DN PLACE OFF
X OEW NR. 12053461
5842/SUP NR. 12053
55842
D KINGDOM NR. 12052
LONDON

NEUHAUS INC.
120 FAIRCHILD AVENU
US-NY 11803 516 57
TEL +001 516 57
UNITED STATES OF
PO NR 2317/25

NEW Y

FI-GI SAS
VIA SAN VI
IT-20123
TEL +003
ITALIA
PRODUITO
PROD.

CAF NEUHAUS
UNIONINKATU 32
HELSINKI 9/66 26
FI-00100
TEL +00358
FINLAND
FAX DD 25/05/07
FAX DD 25/05/07

EL CORTE INGLES C
DPTO 599
VAL DE MORO 06
ES-28009 VALDE
TEL +0034 1
ESPANA
PROVEEDOR 825
PTO0209-9066

FIN

FIN

the managing director of Neuhaus. In 2006, Compagnie du Bois Sauvage made a takeover bid to acquire the remaining Neuhaus shares and by the end of the year, they had acquired all the shares. Neuhaus is thus one of the rare chocolate makers of Belgian origin to have remained securely established as part of the country's heritage.

Today, the tradition of quality and the prestige of the company's creations continue. Great care is taken to maintain the craftsmanship that is essential in the creation of chocolate, while evolving in a world of continuous challenges.

There is a research and development department that studies and tests new raw materials to broaden the gustative palette of pralines and chocolates. The department is also constantly seeking new manufacturing techniques to develop ever more innovative creations while always respecting the tradition.

In 2007, Neuhaus will be celebrating a youthful 150 years of activity and although points of sale have multiplied in Berlin, Hong Kong, London, Madrid, Milan, New York, Paris, Sao Paulo, Singapore and Tokyo, (1,400 stores abroad and almost 100 in Belgium alone!), the boutique in the Galerie de la Reine remains a focal point of great interest.

→ Neuhaus Boutique interior, Galerie de la Reine, Brussels.

The Discovery of Chocolate

A successful evolution in aesthetics!

With the approach of the new century, there was a need to reflect on the presentation of Neuhaus products. How should things be changed, how can Neuhaus attract a new generation of lovers of good chocolate, without upsetting a loyal clientele and renouncing a tradition of 150 years? This is always a difficult exercise but it is now clear that it has proved a brilliant success. Several elements were the driving force behind this change: of course, an ageing brand, its austerity and its tradition firmly anchored in the green and gold, which are often the colours chosen by very new companies seeking to give their products a traditional image; but also the Napoleon myth starting from his style of being beaten at the breach and then recouped by history; or even being blocked by an Asian clientele, a market with a major growth trend but where the colour green is never associated with food. Hugues Tomeo, senior brand manager at Neuhaus, explained, "We have chosen brown, a colour that adapts perfectly to our chocolate colour codes, this is the basic colour. We have added to this generic colour a 'gustative' tone: coral red, which contributes many positive elements such as warmth and dynamism, and which is also becoming a recognisable sign, the emblem of Neuhaus stores. These stores are filled with good humour, energy, youthfulness and love! And not only the stores, but all the packaging has taken on a youthful air and is being regenerated: the setting of our pralines is enhanced and has become more luxurious. To quote Alphonse Karr in *Les Guêpes* 'Plus ça change, plus c'est la même chose', *(The more things change, the more they stay the same)*, we are presenting our tradition in a contemporary language. For 'Créateur chocolatier' and '1857', we have kept the originality of the writing which was written in chocolate! The Neuhaus 'N' has been modernised. This has been followed through for the 'ballotins', tins and ribbons, and also in our boutiques worldwide."

← Symbols of the new Neuhaus identity: the coral red colour and the 'Candles and Spirits' light.

→ Neuhaus store in Bruges.

2

yndia mexicana

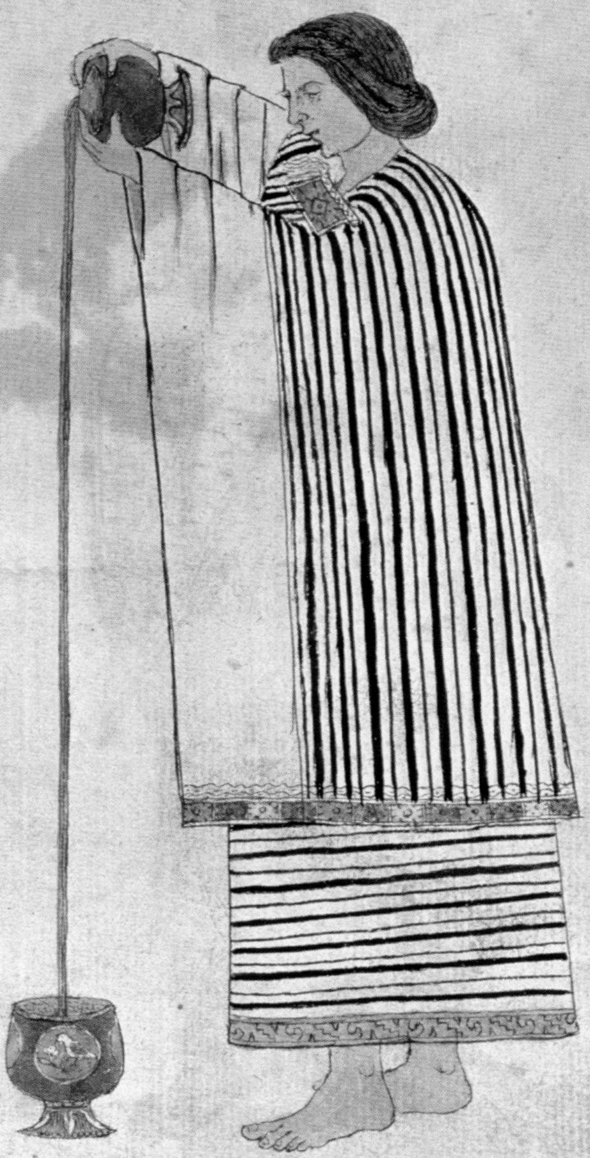

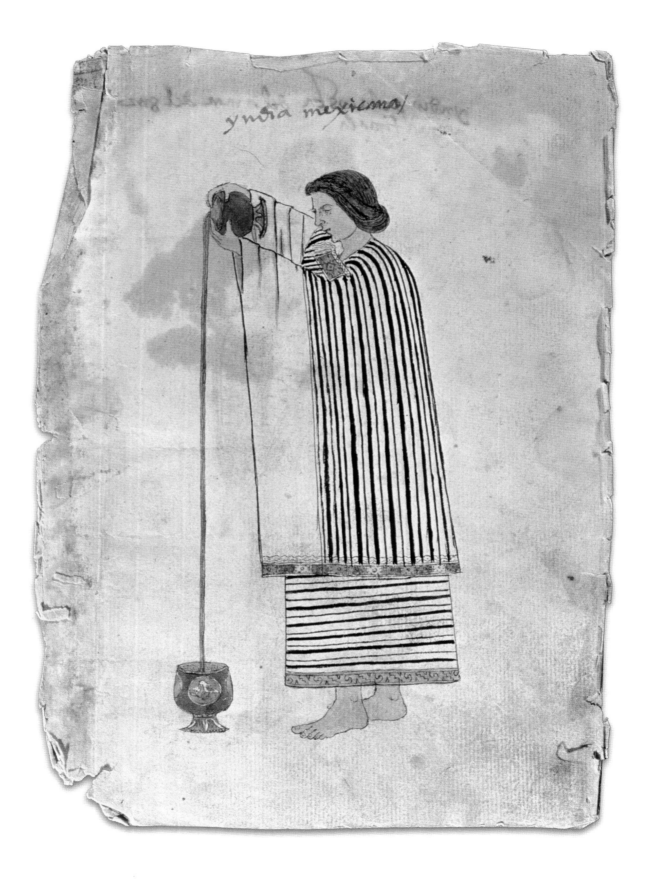

Christopher Columbus

It was during his fourth and last expedition that Christopher Columbus discovered the cocoa bean. Christopher Columbus, probably born in Genoa, Italy, in 1451, sought to take up the challenge of crossing the Atlantic to reach India. He was influenced by reading *Livre des merveilles du monde* (*The book of the wonders of the world*) by the Englishman Sir John Mandeville, written in 1355, and of which only 250 copies were distributed on the Continent. Columbus had the audacious dream of "reaching the east by going west". The navigator sought support and funding from powerful people. The Portuguese monarch, Dom João refused his request; he then turned to Isabella of Castile (Isabella the Catholic) and King Ferdinand II. After much hesitation, and following the insistence of their advisers who spelled out the possible economic advantages, The Catholic monarchs finally funded Columbus's expedition. Isabella and Ferdinand were to launch the Inquisition with all its appalling consequences. They were the initiators of the unification of Spain, which was achieved in the next century. They bequeathed the country to their grandson, Charles V, who as Charles I was to be the first king of a united Spain.

The first voyage of Columbus inaugurated the modern history of the route between the American continent and Europe, and also of the colonisation of America by Europeans. On 3 August 1492, Columbus sailed from the port of Palos de la Frontera (Huelva) with three ships – the Niña, the Pinta and the Santa Maria, and a crew of 90. On 12 October 1492, after a long crossing with many difficulties, storms, rebellions and much discouragement, land came into sight. Christopher Columbus gave this land the name of Christ: San Salvador (Guanahani). This was the very first contact with the natives whom Columbus called "Indians", as he believed he was landing in India.

Comme les Indiens coupent & traittent le Sucre.

→ Indians cutting and treating sugar. *World Gallery*, Leide, s.d., [*circa* 1710], t. 64, plate 33a. Royal Library of Belgium, Brussels.

It was only on his fourth voyage that Columbus discovered the cocoa bean. After Martinique, he landed on the island of Guanaja in 1502, close to the borders of present day Honduras. The island chief wore a headdress decorated with multicolour feathers, which was poetically called "the shadow of Lords and Kings"! It was Ferdinand, the son of Christopher Columbus, who described the scene: a pirogue carved out of a single tree trunk with 25 rowers approached them, loaded with all kinds of merchandise, "many 'almonds' used as money in New Spain (report of 1537) which the natives considered very important. Some of these 'almonds' fell in the water and the natives anxiously tried to scoop them up, as though they had lost an eye!" Columbus did not understand the importance of these 'almonds', which did indeed serve as the local currency. One thousand beans were worth 3 ducats (of Venetian gold) and Columbus's sailors discovered that, for example, a slave could be bought for 100 beans!

Christopher Columbus died in 1506 in Valladolid, fabulously wealthy, Viceroy of India, yet alone and forgotten by his contemporaries.

The Conquistadores

Thanks to his earlier voyages, Christopher Columbus enabled colonisers to be sent to the area and they became settlers. He had opened the way, and very soon, the route to chocolate. Expeditions were organised to conquer the new lands and to evangelise the natives. The troop leaders were explorers, adventurers and missionaries rolled into one, and they called themselves Conquistadores (the Spanish word for 'conquerors'), which is reminiscent of the Spanish word 'reconquista' evoking the reconquering of the Spanish territories occupied by the Moors. During the 15th, 16th and 17th centuries, they seized immense territories in Latin America. It was often impoverished nobles, hidalgos, and mercenaries with no scruples, who wanted to enrich themselves in 'the Indies', since they were unable to do so in Europe. There were rumours of the existence of entire cities built of gold which encouraged them

↓ Hernán Cortés sent the first cocoa beans to Spain. A. Thévet, *Portraits and lives of famous men*, Paris, 1584, plate 385. Royal Library of Belgium, Brussels.

to set forth: a marvellous city called Cibola was said to exist in North America and another called Eldorado in South America. Several expeditions were launched to find these cities, but they always returned with less gold than they had expected. The colonisation was brutal, local sovereigns were eliminated by the more sophisticated European weaponry. Very few troops were needed, but those who were there showed great determination. Other fortuitous circumstances also helped their cause, such as the propagation of hitherto unknown diseases which decimated local populations. Thus Juan Ponce de León conquered Porto Rico, Diego Velasquez occupied Cuba and Vasco Nuñez de Balboa invaded Panama. In Peru, it was Diego de Almagro and Francisco Pizarro who became the masters, while Hernán Cortés landed in Mexico, then Honduras and southern California.

In 1519, Hernán Cortés disembarked on the Mexican coast. He was at the head of an army of 700 soldiers,

equipped with horses and canons. That same year, Charles V, born in Ghent in 1500, was made Holy Roman Emperor, on the death of his grandfather. He was also King of Germany, King of Spain and of Spanish America... and Duke of Brabant. In 1520, Cortés wrote his first report to the king which stated, "The natives set great store by the cocoa beans; they treat them like currency throughout their lands and use them to purchase everything they need in the markets". At first the Spaniards were disappointed not to receive gold, however, they very quickly understood how they could take advantage of this local asset. The Mayan system of calculation was vigesimal, in other words, it had the number 20 as its base. The Mayan calendar was also governed by the same rules, with the day as the base. Each one of the 20 days had a god as its patron and was itself a divinity with its attributes. Thus the day "manik" is associated with the parrot, blood and the cocoa bean! It was discovered that 400 beans (20 times 20) were worth 1 tzontli, 20 tzontlis (8,000 beans) were worth 1 xiquipilli; 3 xiquipillis were worth 1 carga, i.e. 24,000 cocoa beans. Five years later, Cortés sent to his Emperor and King the very first

↑ Hernán Cortés being greeted by the Aztec Emperor Montezuma II. Don Antonio de Solis, *History of the Conquest of Mexico*, Brussels, 1741, plate 135. Royal Library of Belgium, Brussels.

cargo of cocoa beans, and it was said that Charles V was delighted with the beverage, as was his entire court. However, cocoa beans not only had trading value, primarily they had a religious and then culinary significance.

Quetzalcoatl

The Indians have a legend about the origin of cocoa. There are parallels with myths in other civilisations and other religions. Bernardino de Sahagun, a Franciscan, transcribed the following text:

"Quetzalcoatl was highly regarded and perceived as a god; he was adored in ancient times in Tollan. He had a very ugly face, a long head and he wore a beard. His vassals were able craftsmen who could cut green stones, called chalchihuites, melt silver and do many other things; all these arts were said to come from Quetzalcoatl himself. He had houses made of precious green stones, and others made of silver, white and coloured shells, turquoises and other precious stones. It was also said that he was very rich, that he had everything he needed for food and drink, that the corn was very abundant, and that the cotton was harvested in many different colours. It was also said that the people of Tula bred all kinds of birds with coloured plumage, and that there were other birds that sang harmoniously. Quetzalcoatl had all the riches in the world, gold, silver, precious stones and other items of value, and an abundance of cocoa trees, which were called "xochicacaoatl". Then the time came when the fortune of Quetzalcoatl and of the Toltecs was gone. Three sorcerers came to Tula and spread many lies. The magician Titlacauan came to Quetzalcoatl disguised as a hoary old man and said to him, "My Lord, I bring you a potion that is good, that intoxicates the person who drinks it; it will melt your heart, it will heal you and help you know the route of your next voyage to the land of Tlapallan, where you will become young again." And Quetzalcoatl drank the potion, was intoxicated and lost his head. He decided to leave Tula for the land of Tlapallan; he burned all his houses made of silver and of shells, he buried the other precious items in the mountains and river beds, and transformed the cocoa trees into another species of tree called "mizquitl". He sent before him all the species of birds with colourful plumage and he left Tula travelling in the direction of the rising sun..."

↓ The serpent god Quetzalcoatl possessed many riches, including an abundance of cocoa trees. Mexico, the Aztec culture, 1250-1521. Quai Branly Museum, Paris.

The Mayas kept their cocoa beans in sacred vases which formed part of the funeral offerings of high dignitaries. The glyph, a drawing representing "kawkaw", has been found on many urns. As for the cocoa growers, they had a special adoration for a god with a black face and a long nose called Ek Chuah. According to the Mayas, the earth was situated between the 13 celestial levels and the 9 infernal layers. Each of the cardinal points was associated with a deity, a cosmic tree, a bird, etc. A variety of the cocoa tree was thus found at each of the four cardinal points planted during the dark ages to indicate the path leading to the light.

↑ Zoomorphic vase of the 'chocolate pot' model, Mexico, Huaxtec culture, 1200-1521. Royal Museums of Art and History, Brussels.

→ Cocoa pod, Mayan culture (?), pre-Hispanic period, Mexico or Guatemala. Royal Museums of Art and History, Brussels.

The legend recounts that Quetzalcoatl left on a raft and drifted along the Tabasco coast towards the rising sun, and it was at this precise location that the fleet of Hernán Cortés appeared! The men's uniforms and their shining feathered helmets lent credence to the native belief that they were the incarnation of ancient gods and of Quetzalcoatl! They made this legend their own (We are the descendants of the kingdom of Toltec and of Quetzalcoatl!); all the more so since it legitimized the invasion of the Mexicas (later called the Aztecs), which had taken place around 1300 in the present day Mexican valley. These invaders created a new empire which extended as far as the border with the Mayas, who occupied the Yucatan peninsula. It is still not understood why the big Mayan cities were abandoned by their inhabitants towards the end of the 9th century. The last Mayan dynasty of the Cocomes still levied a tribute of cocoa beans on 20 or so small impoverished villages.

Montezuma II

The emperor who received Cortés in 1519 was called Montezuma II. He lived in his palace in the town of Tenochtitlán, which was large, well structured, "well thought out" today's town planners would say. The town was dominated by an immense temple, the Teocalli, built on a pyramid of 114°. In 1521, the Spaniards destroyed the entire town and reduced the inhabitants to a state of slavery, i.e. only two years after their invasion! Europeans repopulated the area, they were impatient to make their fortunes, and this presence subsequently gave rise to the birth of Mexico.

Montezuma II owned large cocoa tree plantations.
A. Thévet, *Portraits and lives of famous men,* Paris, 1584, plate 644. Royal Library of Belgium, Brussels.

Montezuma held the cocoa bean in great esteem. He owned vast plantations of cocoa trees, a sign of his religious and earthly power. But what is the origin of the word 'chocolate'? The word designating the cocoa bean in Mayan is 'cacau', in *Nahuatl*, the local Aztec language, it is 'cacauatl' and the drink obtained after grinding the bean 'chacau haa' is called 'chocoatl'. We will return to this theme.

Gonzalo Fernandez de Oviedo gave the recipe for chocolate in his book *Historia general y natural de las Indias* in 1530: take 30 beans to 1 quart of water; roast them and grind finely; add some rocou (a reddish orange pigment), which makes the powder look like human blood. It is drunk, cold, warm or hot. Mix with hallucinogenic mushrooms and lots of spices, in particular bombax seeds and pepper! This is a stimulating drink and should only be given to war lords and their leader, the emperor himself. He adores this strong drink which gives him "a desire to go with women"! It is also invigorating. The chronicler Bernard Diaz del Castillo wrote: "When you have a drink of chocolate, you can travel all day without feeling tired and without feeling a need to consume any other food." He also described the importance of drinking chocolate with meals: "At banquets, you can see more than 50 large earthenware jars containing good chocolate with its froth." Bernardino de Sahagun related: "The person selling the chocolate drink must first grind the beans with the initial rough grinding only crushing the beans; then the second grinding is finer; the third and last grinding is the finest, mixing the powder with well washed cooked corn grains. Once this has been done, it should be put into a vase with water; if there is a small quantity, no froth is produced. In order that the beverage be correctly prepared, it should first be sieved.

It must then be poured from a height so that froth is formed as it is poured. Sometimes, it can be too thick, water should then be added. The chocolate drink maker who prepares it well can also sell it for a good price when it has a good aspect, such as the nobility drink; it is sweet, frothy, vermilion in colour, with no mixture and no lumps. Aromatic spices are sometimes added, even bee's honey and a little rose water. A bad drinking chocolate is lumpy and contains a lot of water; it is runny and does not form any froth."

A metate is used for the grinding, this is a rectangular grinding slab, curved inwards on one side and resting on three legs. Europeans did not drink very much chocolate until, forced by a shortage of wine and not wanting to drink water, they tried it. Girolamo Benzoni, a mercenary from Milan said of the drink, "Chocoatl should be thrown to the pigs!" Gonzalo Fernandez de Oviedo described drinking it as follows: "The cocoa powder is mixed with a little water to make a thick paste that is set aside. This paste can be used to prepare a drink; or it can also be applied to the face so that one appears to be covered in mud, some people even look very red because of the rocou. With their faces covered with this paste, they go to the market or elsewhere and from time to time they suck a little of this oil with their fingers. We Christians find this a very dirty habit, yet they do not find it disgust-

↑ V. Zelensky, *A cocoa tree bearing several cocoa pods with fruit strewn at the foot of the tree*. Quai Branly Museum, Paris.

→ Goblet with painted decoration, Mayan culture, Guatemala or Mexico, 600-900 (kakawa glyph). Royal Museums of Art and History (a gift presented by Smets), Brussels.

ing at all, in fact quite the contrary, they find it useful, as they do not feel thirsty or hungry and it protects their faces from the sun and air." On the other hand, the Dominican friar Pedro Martyr de Angleria regularly informed Pope Clement VII of the peculiar things seen in the New World. He wrote of the chocolate drink in these terms: "Oh, fortunate currency that provides the human race with such a delicious and useful potion, keeping those who possess it free from the infernal plague of avarice since it cannot be buried or kept for a long time!"

We now know that cocoa originated in the basins of the Orinoco (Venezuela) and the Amazon (Brazil). It was an island situated at the mouth of the Orinoco where Robinson Crusoe, the legendary hero of Daniel Defoe's book (1719), survived for 28 years! The Amazon is the world's biggest river, in length, flow and area of its basin. It was from these hot and humid regions that the cocoa tree spread to neighbouring territories. The oldest varieties of cocoa bean, the "criollo", "forastero" and the "nacional ecuatoriano", all came from a single nursery. In the 13th century before our era, the Olmecs (one of the most ancient American civilisations established in the tropical jungle of the Gulf of Mexico between 2000 B.C. and 500 B.C.) already cultivated the cocoa trees. There is proof that they drank hot chocolate at least six centuries before the Christian era, since a pot containing traces of cocoa was discovered in Belize (former British Honduras).

Hernán Cortés asked Montezuma to plant 2,000 cocoa trees and demanded that the profits be sent to the Emperor Charles V. He surveyed the 40,000 reserve loads belonging to Montezuma. When local governments were abolished and colonial authority had been established, the Spaniards understood that cocoa could also be a source of great profits, in addition to the silver, by levying taxes on the Indians.

Maniere dont les habitans de la nouvelle Espagne preparent le Cacao pour le Chocolat.

Juan de Zumàrraga

The Spanish started to drink chocolate and it really became part of their customs. Thus, when celebrating the peace signed between Charles V and François I in 1538, the viceroy Antonio de Mendoza organised a great banquet in the Burgundy tradition where chocolate was served. It was recounted that the president of the Supreme Court and all the civil servants working there had become accustomed to drinking chocolate. The Spanish immigrants who frequented the homes of Indians also drank chocolate. In the silver mines, the merchants offered chocolate as well as their textiles. Cocoa was also used as medication for stomach ache and chest pains. Moreover, the pomade was used for chapped lips or cracked nipples. The story was told that in the virgin forest, the Italian cook of Fernandez de Oviedo, whose name was Nicolà, had prepared a meal for him consisting of eggs and fish, fried in cocoa oil... However, it was with Juan de Zumàrraga that the infatuation was born. The name of this Franciscan archbishop of Mexico, Juan de Zumàrraga, is not as well known as that of Montezuma; nevertheless, it is he who was responsible for that extra impetus that opened the route of chocolate to Europe: the mixture of sugar and cocoa. Before Juan de Zumàrraga, the cocoa beans, even roasted ground and mixed with various liquids, did not please the European palate. The Spanish had planted sugar cane in the Canaries, Santo Domingo and Mexico. A community of nuns in Oaxaca discovered by chance these recipes created for their archbishop, an alchemy mixture of cocoa and sugar. Sometimes they also added aniseed or cinnamon. Because of this tasty mixture, chocolate finally entered the world of European gastronomy to play an essential role, which continues today.

However, the cocoa bean was not introduced into other areas of the world, unlike tobacco, sweet peppers, tomatoes or even manioc. The cocoa bean remained the strong element of Spanish trade for a long time, even after the adoption of other foodstuffs such as coffee and sugar by the English and the French. Though the pineapple was found to be the most delicious fruit of America, everyone agreed that the cocoa bean was the most useful and the most profitable. It was known as the "voluptuous life blood of the New World".

← How the inhabitants of New Spain prepared the cacau (*sic*) to make chocolate. *World Gallery*, Leide, s.d., [*circa* 1710], t. 63, plate 17. Royal Library of Belgium, Brussels.

↓ Molinillo (cocoa beater), Mexico. Quai Branly Museum, Paris.

The Chocolate Route

NOUVELLE ESPAGNE,
NOUVELLE GALICE,
et
GUATIMALA,
dans
l'Amerique Septentrionale,
suivant les Mémoires de ceux qui en on fait
la decouverte, recemment mis au jour par
PIERRE VANDER AA,
Marchand Libraire A LEIDE.

Lieues d'Allemagne de 15 au Degré.
Lieues de France de 20 au Degré.

GOLFO DE NU[
ESPAÑA

Terlichichimechi

Costa
Baxa

el
hincon

NUEVA BISCAYA

NUEVA LEON

PANVCO

ZACATECAS

NUEVA GALICIA

NUEVA
ESPAÑA

MAR DEL ZV[

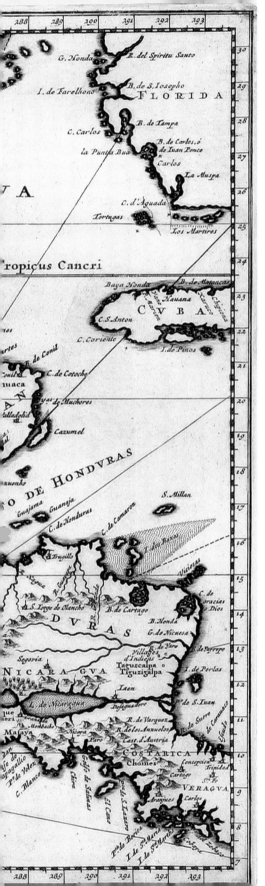

Mexico, the number one country for chocolate

From the beginning of the 17th century, chocolate was a national beverage in Mexico. It was drunk twice a day: in the morning between seven and eight o'clock, and in the late afternoon between five and six o'clock. Chocolate sauce could even accompany a roast turkey! All sorts of mixtures with a chocolate base were sold on the street. A refreshing version was a mixture of chocolate and atole, a gruel made with corn; another mixture was made of chocolate and 'leche de gallina', a liqueur made from natural benjoin resin. There was a difference between the European mixtures which used cinnamon, pepper, aniseed, or a sort of sesame seed called ajonjoli and the Indian mixtures which were chocolate with gueynacaztle, with its sweet fragrance, or tlixochil, vanilla, achiote, tegument of bixia fruits with their beautiful red colour, or grilled sweet peppers and chili peppers. It is said that chocolate sharpens the appetite, that the cocoa bean eaten raw helps the digestion; there are so many sayings! There are many reports referring to the high consumption of chocolate during that period. Thus, the Flemish Jesuit Thomas van Hamme, who travelled to Mexico in 1687, asserted that everyone who could afford it drank chocolate every day. Gemelli Careri, a navigator who stopped over at the port of Acapulco, recounted that he and all his crew were given chocolate twice a day. During an expedition in the port area, he described how

← Map of New Spain and Guatemala in northern America. *World Gallery*, Leide, s.d., [*circa* 1710], t. 63, plate 6. Royal Library of Belgium, Brussels.

← Page 58: *Cocoa plantation on the island of Grenada.* O'Shea Gallery, London.

61

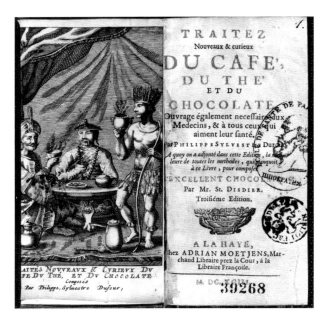

↑ Philippe Sylvestre Dufour, *New and unusual treatise on coffee, tea and chocolate*, Den Haag, 1693.

↓ Posture of a man making chocolate paste. *Good customs for the use of tea, coffee and chocolate in preserving the wellbeing and curing the sick*, Paris, 1687, p. 247. National Library of France, Paris.

the banks were covered with small stalls where the Indians sold chocolate mixed with atole and tamales. He also noticed sugar or chocolate cubes bearing images of religious figures. The ones called 'calaveras' were the death heads that were eaten on All Souls' Day. This became one of the curiosities of Mexican folklore.

Elsewhere, the consumption of chocolate was supplanted by tea, particularly among the Jesuits who drank yerba-mate. Among the Spanish colonies, it was only the Philippines, which was partly a dependency of Mexico, that followed the movement. A certain Carlo van der Haegen, born in Eeklo, Flanders, who joined the East India Company after an unhappy love affair, confirmed that chocolate was proving a huge success in Manila. For example, a French Jesuit had invited him to drink a cup of chocolate after mass!

One century later, there are documents substantiating the continued popularity of chocolate in Mexico, as can be seen in the writings of the Capuchin Francisco de Ajofrîn in 1763. Valets, shoemakers, mule-drivers and coachmen all drank chocolate twice a day and it contained the most costly ingredients, some of them even drank chocolate four times a day or more. There were social and regional differences reflected in how the chocolate was preferred: the Indians drank it cold, while the Creoles drank it hot, but they did not boil it. The Capuchin, finding the chocolate drunk in Europe better, deduced that as with wine, crossing the ocean improved the quality. He also described the cocoa tree plantations at Oaxa, which provided a living for 80 native families. However, the Mexican production was soon not enough and additional cocoa bean production had to be developed in countries that were dependent on Mexico: the coastal area of present day Guatemala, Salvador, Honduras and even Costa Rica. Corn was traded for cocoa beans. As for Venezuela, it seems that it was the country's largest town, Caracas, where the best cocoa beans were produced. There were many Spanish citizens among the traders who became very rich, notably Pieter de Blancke of Bruges, whose son Pedro established himself in business and exported cocoa beans to the Flemish-Sevillano trader Nicolas Antonio.

Spain goes mad for chocolate

It is generally agreed that it was in the 1590s that all of Spain became infatuated with chocolate, even though it had been known there for decades. The aristocrats set the tone and the rest of the population imitated them and became big consumers of chocolate. Jean-Antoine Coget, of Antwerp, travelling in Cadiz at the time, noted in his report that the valets drank portions of the beverage that were two or three times bigger than their masters' portions. This gave rise to the expression *"ni le dejó un bollo de chocolate"* - *"he didn't even leave him one chocolate ball".* Indeed, chocolate was used to prepare drinks, ice creams and pastries. Moreover, it became customary to dunk small rolls into drinking chocolate, which then became consistent due to the milk, vanilla and egg yolk – but this was completely against the rules of etiquette! This enthusiasm for chocolate was perceived by foreigners as a sign of decadence, and it was a very expensive habit. The viceroy of Navarre declared in 1651 to the British ambassador that every year he spent between 2,000 and 3,000 ducats on chocolate. In 1774, the price of one pound of good quality chocolate in Seville cost four times the costs of a Dutch cheese and twice the salary of an unskilled worker! Moralisers such as Francisco de Quevedo, came out against what they called *"el Diablo del chocolate"* – *"the chocolate demon".* The temptation was already there...

Many artisans were able to live from this mania for chocolate: potters, coppersmiths and silversmiths. There was even an activity whereby a craftsman came to the home to grind cocoa beans. The chocolate route linking New Spain, America and Europe was very prosperous, so much so that the popularity of cocoa soon enabled Spain to invade the rest of the old continent! It is worth noting that until this time, the Spanish had jealously guarded the trade monopoly for themselves and especially the secret of how to produce chocolate, reserved for aristocrats and the religious orders. As Flanders and the Netherlands were Spanish territories in the 16th century, it was these regions that were the first to receive Spanish chocolate exports.

↓ Slaves preparing the chocolate during a stop in the journey of Spanish travellers, 19th century, Archives of the national Manufacture of Sèvres.

The Queens of Chocolate

Two queens of France brought the fashion for drinking chocolate with them from their countries of origin. The first one was the Infanta of Spain, Anne of Austria who married Louis XIII in 1615. On the death of the king in 1643, she became regent and asserted her love of chocolate. Cardinal Mazarin even brought a chocolate maker from Turin and engaged him on his personnel staff. The second chocolate-loving queen was the Infanta Maria Theresa of Austria who married Louis XIV in 1660. The chroniclers of the time wrote that the only two passions of Maria Theresa were the king and... chocolate. The king himself declared it was a food that tricked hunger but did not fill the stomach. At Versailles, chocolate was served in the salons every Monday, Wednesday and Thursday. After the death of Maria Theresa, Louis married Madame de Maintenon and she stipulated that chocolate be served at the sumptuous festivities at Marly and Versailles. The aristocrats emulated the royal household and also served chocolate. To return to the Infanta Anna, one could not help but notice one of her courtiers, known as the "Molina" because she was responsible for using the small whisk that she turned in the chocolate cup so that the drink was nice and frothy!

What did the chocolate service look like, given that it differed from a tea service or a coffee service? It was made up of a chocolate pot with a whisk and chocolate cups. Good chocolate pots had to be balloon-shaped and were generally made of copper and silver, with a handle in wood or ivory. They measured approximately 30 cm in height. Earthenware chocolate pots, for example, once they were heated allowed the bubbles to rise to the surface and the chocolate boiled over! The cups were porcelain. The whisk was an accessory that formed part of the chocolate pot: it was made from a hard wood and was called a froth maker, stirrer, whisk, or notched rod (it resembled a pine cone). It had to be rolled between the palms of the hand in order to stir the liquid. There was also an addition to the usual service, the "tremblers"; these were saucers onto which cups had been fixed so that an elderly and trembling guest would not drop or lose any of the precious liquid!

← Luis Meléndez, *Still life with chocolate pot*, 1776. Prado Museum, Madrid.

↓ Meissen china trembleuse, mid-19th century. Barry Callebaut, Chocolate Museum, Eupen.

In 1659, David Chaillou became the first official chocolate maker in France. A royal decree of 1705 authorised vendors of soft drinks to sell drinking chocolate too. In the 18th century, chocolate became extremely fashionable and more and more people became involved in the chocolate sector, inventors, traders, consumers, etc. In 1732, Dubuisson invented a horizontal table heated with charcoal which made it easier to prepare the chocolate. In 1778, Doret invented the first hydraulic machine for grinding cocoa beans.

The favourites of Louis XV were enthusiastic about chocolate for different reasons. Madame de Pompadour used it "to become hot-blooded", as the king had said that she was "a cold fish". Madame du Barry offered chocolate to her lovers so that they would satisfy her; she had an insatiable lust.

The round of queens continued with Marie-Antoinette who married Louis XVI in 1770. She came from Austria accompanied by her personal chocolate maker, who prepared chocolate for the queen mixed with sugar and vanilla, and also other more elaborate recipes such as chocolate mixed with an orchid bulb for strength, chocolate with orange blossom to calm the nerves, or chocolate with sweet almond milk to aid the digestion. Marie-Antoinette created the position of "Chocolate Maker to the Queen", an office far more lucrative than many baronies with their proudly emblazoned gyronny.

Bayonne, the cradle of chocolate in France

In a manner somewhat parallel to the official entry of chocolate in France through the intermediary of the queens, Bayonne really became the true cradle of chocolate in France. Jews fleeing the Inquisition had to leave Spain and then Portugal; some settled in Bayonne in 1496. They took refuge in the port towns of the Atlantic, more precisely the small village of Saint-Esprit, on the banks of the river Adour. They brought with them the secrets of chocolate that they knew. They opened the first chocolate boutique in 1580! In 1610, they established a chocolate manufacturing plant there. The people of Bayonne were initiated into the production of this food of the gods and they became the first artisans in the kingdom of France to work with the cocoa bean. The guild of chocolate makers and wax makers was formed. Many Bayonne families perpetuated the chocolate making tradition from that time: Biraben, Etchepare and Dominique, who set up establishments in rue Pannecau, Cazenave, Guillot, Daranatz... and for the chocolate making workshops: Fagalde, Harispe or Noblia in Cambo. By 1822, there were more than 20 artisans working in the Bayonne area and by 1830, there were 130 chocolate workers, more than in Switzerland!

In the 20th century, industrialisation supplanted Bayonne's position, yet the tradition continues in the Basque country and today there are some 15 local enterprises with more than 200 employees. Two chocolate factories and five pastry and chocolate makers forming a guild have been brought together by the Academy of Chocolate. The Academy of Chocolate and the Chocolate Makers Guild, founded in 1993 to promote its reputation, have put together the history of Bayonne chocolate through a series of archives. This guild created the museum of chocolate in Biarritz. The French certificate of professional aptitude for chocolate making and the ratification of a diploma of the techniques of the profession were created and implemented by the Chamber of Professions of the Pyrénées-Atlantiques region. One of the pastries of the region is called "the Basque beret" and is

← Firmin Buisset, poster for Menier chocolate, 1893. Private collection.

↑ Jean-Charles Develly, *The chocolate maker 'The Loyal Ones'*, 1820-1835. National Ceramic Museum, Sèvres.

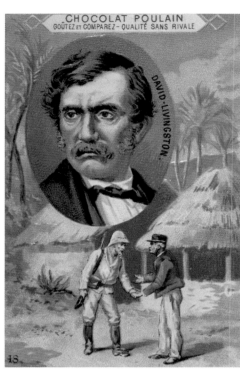

made of a chocolate sponge cake, a chocolate ganache, a syrup that is 16° proof, all coated in dark chocolate, chocolate vermicelli and a dash of Grand Marnier!

In the 19th century, the French were the champions of medicinal forms of chocolate which were made by pharmacists. There were preparations for analeptic, bechic (for coughs), and pectoral conditions, and chocolate preparations for stomach problems, osmazome-based, magnesium purgative chocolate and even tar-based chocolate!

In the industrial era, the great names in the history of French chocolate were Menier, Poulain and Barry. Jean-Antoine Brutus Menier launched the chocolate tablet in 1836 at Noisiel. There was a facsimile of an official medal and his signature on the wrapping, as a commitment to the client; this was a first in the history of commerce. Menier was also the first company to place advertisements in the newspapers, by publishing a catalogue. In 1844, the company had 800 clients and 75 employees. Menier purchased land in Nicaragua. A fleet of ships was built there to transport cocoa beans, including the famous vessel "Belem". In 1906, Menier launched milk chocolate and in 1913, a milk chocolate fondant called "Lugano". In 1928, there was a memorable Art Deco poster in 1928 of a 'tomboy' wearing an attractive Coco Chanel design. In 1960, Cacao-Barry acquired a stake in Menier. In 1848, Victor-Auguste Poulain, a Blois confectioner, launched his first chocolate tablets coated with fine gold leaf. 1848 remains the company's most appreciated collection. 1848 was the year of universal suffrage and the election of the first President of the Republic. Poulain's aim was to change the perception of chocolate as a health product to a pleasurable food. It appears that the first chocolates were made in the house where the famous magician Jean-Eugène Robert-Houdin was born. From 1863, posters with a background in the French national colours, red, white and blue were distributed, announcing "Taste and Compare"! In 1884, Albert Poulain, son of the founder, invented the "breakfast chocolate with vanilla cream" with a surprise gift of little soldiers in the packet! Always at the forefront of innovative advertising, Poulain launched chromos in 1880. By 1900, more than 300,000 were sold every day. Poulain also revolutionised the market introducing chocolate 'powder', orange flavoured chocolate and the family size chocolate bar. In 1898, Poulain launched "cocoa powder for an instant breakfast" which could be stirred into any boiling liquid. In 1990, an ultra-modern factory was designed by the architect Jean Nouvel and one-third of France's population were drinking Poulain cocoa.

↑ Advertising image for Poulain chocolate, The Easter Eggs, 20th century. Museum of Popular Art and Traditions, Paris.

Charles Barry founded his chocolate factory in 1842 in England and established a presence in France in 1920. In 1996, the company became Barry-Callebaut. Callebaut was founded in Belgium in 1850, but produced its first chocolate bars in 1911.

In France today, there are still the great traditional chocolate establishments, such as Maurice Bernachon of Lyon, "La Marquise de Sévigné" founded in Auvergne by Clémentine and Auguste Rouzaud in 1898, the chocolate desserts of Pierre Hermé, the chocolate cellars of Jean-Paul Hévin, and the "Maison du Chocolat" opened in Paris in 1977 by Robert Linxe – in general, they specialise in dark chocolate.

Dark chocolate tolerates no compromise, it has a prickly nature; it does not accept alliances, darkly proud, it is soothing but never weak; curt when necessary, penetrating, and somewhat perverse. But the chocolate that is mixed with milk is easily forgotten; like a child, it is fearful, and clings to its mother's skirt. It can turn on the charm. Yet it is a substance ashamed of its own presence, easily pleased, reverting to infancy and a child's world.

(Alain Schiffres)

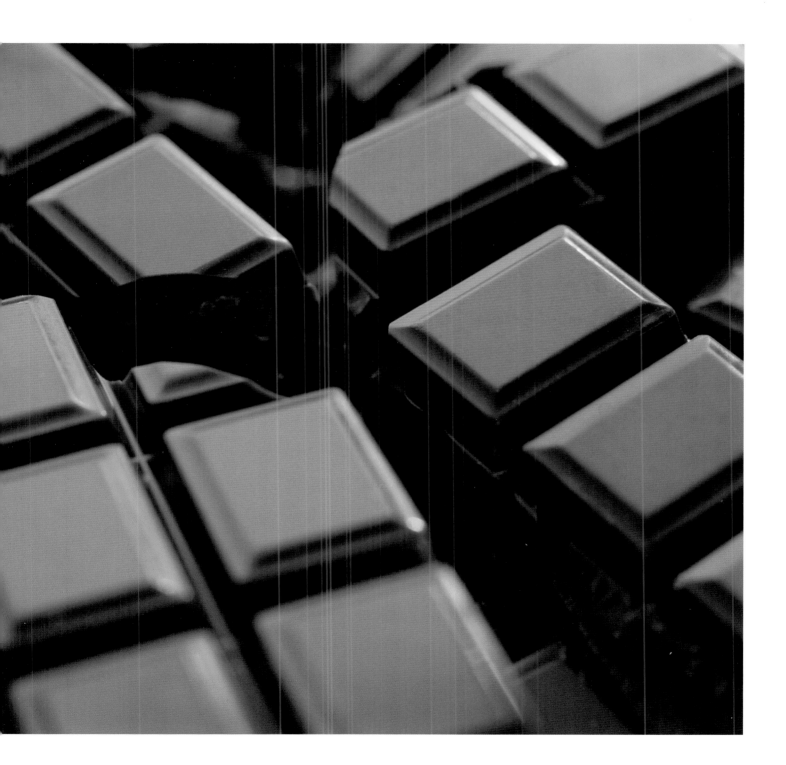

The Italian chocolate makers

The Italian traveller Antonio Carletti drank chocolate in the West Indies, where he stayed; he probably drank it in Spain too where he found himself in 1606. Whatever the case, he noted his impressions in a travel journal and that is why the Italians became enthusiastic about this nectar. The Italians drank their chocolate cold; it is cooled with ice cubes, or with snow. There were chocolate makers everywhere. The first town where chocolate arrived was Perugia, which inspired the famous brand *Perugina*. Still today, Perugia, proud of its past, organises the Perugia Eurochocolate Festival in October. This is an event dedicated to the culture of chocolate, whose very heart is in the historic town centre. The organisers claim it is the chocolate festivity that is the most loved and most closely followed by Italians, and that it has made Perugia the European chocolate capital. The "Baci", little round mouthfuls filled with chocolate paste and grilled crushed hazelnuts, the flagship of the Perugina brand which, since 1922, has enabled Italian boys to send kisses to their sweethearts.

The best known Italian invention dates back to 1867, and that is "gianduja", a triangular twig shaped chocolate with rounded edges, wrapped in gold or silver paper. Gianduja is a mixture made of hazelnuts, sugar and chocolate. The hazelnuts used to come from the nut trees growing wild on the hills south of Turin, which have a particular fragrance. It was an action promoted by the famous FIAT automobile company (FIAT is based in Turin) that introduced this speciality chocolate to the entire world. FIAT had requested that the gianduja be wrapped in paper bearing its brand image and had them sent to every single one of its clients worldwide!

As for the Venetians, they wanted to appropriate the creation of the first boutiques selling chocolate!

← The contemporary version of gianduja chocolate by Neuhaus.

A German evening chocolate

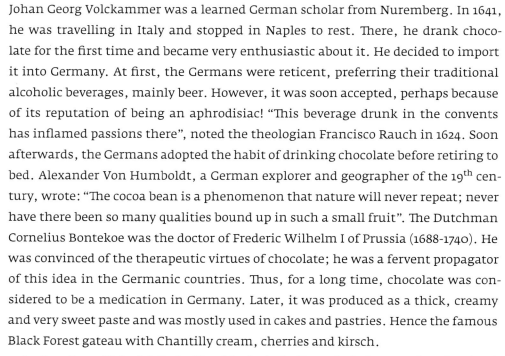

Johan Georg Volckammer was a learned German scholar from Nuremberg. In 1641, he was travelling in Italy and stopped in Naples to rest. There, he drank chocolate for the first time and became very enthusiastic about it. He decided to import it into Germany. At first, the Germans were reticent, preferring their traditional alcoholic beverages, mainly beer. However, it was soon accepted, perhaps because of its reputation of being an aphrodisiac! "This beverage drunk in the convents has inflamed passions there", noted the theologian Francisco Rauch in 1624. Soon afterwards, the Germans adopted the habit of drinking chocolate before retiring to bed. Alexander Von Humboldt, a German explorer and geographer of the 19th century, wrote: "The cocoa bean is a phenomenon that nature will never repeat; never have there been so many qualities bound up in such a small fruit". The Dutchman Cornelius Bontekoe was the doctor of Frederic Wilhelm I of Prussia (1688-1740). He was convinced of the therapeutic virtues of chocolate; he was a fervent propagator of this idea in the Germanic countries. Thus, for a long time, chocolate was considered to be a medication in Germany. Later, it was produced as a thick, creamy and very sweet paste and was mostly used in cakes and pastries. Hence the famous Black Forest gateau with Chantilly cream, cherries and kirsch.

In the 1870s, Heinrich Imhoff and Ludwig Stollwerck, heirs to a chocolate business, invested and innovated and turned their firm into the world's leading chocolate company.

The first chocolate cake recipe was written in Austria in 1778, but it was in 1832 that the master pastry cook of Emperor Franz Joseph created the famous Sacher Torte (named after him) in Vienna. This is a chocolate cake filled with a layer of apricot jam and dark chocolate icing. Later the Imperial Torte recipe would include a mixture of almond paste with milk chocolate.

The English cocoa tree

The first traces of cacao in England date back to 1657. Cacao? That should be Cocoa, since English is the only language in the world in which the name of this food of the gods has been changed! It seems that it was due to pronunciation difficulties and the position of the tongue. In the columns of the newspaper *The Public Advertiser*, one could read, "In Bishopsgate, a delicious beverage coming from the West Indies may be drunk." This drink, in a land of tea drinkers, was considered "extravagant" and in the beginning, it was only consumed by real chocolate lovers. Chocolate was more readily used in pastry making and it was as cakes that it was eaten in 1674 at the 'Coffee Mill and Tobacco Roll'. Several decades later, people became more interested in this exotic food: Henry Sloane devoted a book to the cocoa tree in 1725. Shortly after that, King Georges I levied a tax on the consumption and sale of chocolate, a testimony to the new enthusiasm for chocolate. In 1728, it was seen as a necessity in an industrialised England to have their first chocolate factory with a hydraulic machine, the brainchild of Walter Churchman of Bristol. And, it was England, everything had to go through societies and clubs: in 1746, the Cocoa Tree was founded, a club of chocolate tasters. Experiments were carried out there, such as mixing eggs or wine with chocolate and, of course, replacing water with milk.

In the 19th century, John Cadbury was a major name in chocolate. He also created the workers' city at Bournville, near Birmingham.

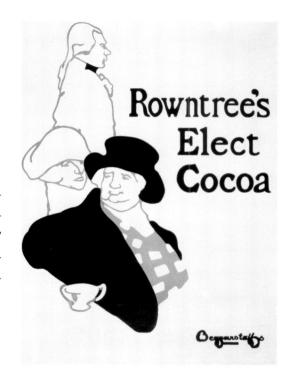

↗ William Nicholson and James Pryde, poster for Rowntree's Elect Cocoa, 1895. Private collection.

→ Advertisement for Cadbury's Cocoa Essence, 1878. Library of Decorative Arts, Paris.

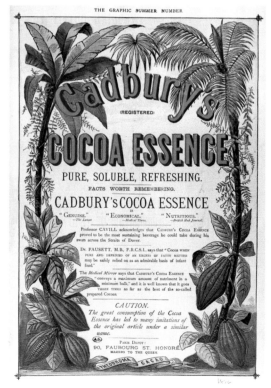

Inventions of the Swiss chocolate makers

As for the discovery of chocolate in Italy by Germans, the same thing occurred when the Swiss discovered chocolate. This important experience took place in an establishment on the famous Grand Place of Brussels, Belgium. In 1697, the establishment served a cup of chocolate to Henri Escher, the mayor of Zurich. He took the recipe with him to his country and thereby initiated the enthusiasm for chocolate in one of the great chocolate countries. Chocolate making started in Switzerland in 1792, the year when Josty headed up a chocolate company in Berne. Yet it was especially in the 19th century that great innovations concerning chocolate appeared in Switzerland. In 1819, François-Louis Caillier opened a first factory at Corsier, near Vevey. The people of Turin claimed to have been the inventors of the technique that enabled the chocolate to solidify and hence be made into bars, because Caillier had been apprenticed to an Italian chocolate maker. While in 1826, Philippe Suchard opened a chocolate factory at Neuchâtel, then another at Serrières; in 1830, Charles-Amédée Kholer founded his own

chocolate factory (where he created chocolate with hazelnuts); in 1868, it was Jean Tobler's turn (the Tobler company used the Italian 'torrone' formula, a mixture of chocolate, honey, egg whites and almonds and the famous three-dimensional triangular bar was created. Today it can be found in every corner of the globe). In 1879, Robert Lindt set up a business in Berne; in 1884, Alexis Séchaud founded his company in Montreux; and in the meantime, in 1875, Daniel Peter developed the technique for making milk chocolate. This mixture of cocoa powder (a Dutch invention from Van Houten) and creamy farm milk, a Swiss speciality, revolutionised the world of chocolate. Inspired by the process developed by Henri Nestlé, Daniel Peter went on to create the formula that combined the milk and the powder. He managed to succeed by using condensed milk. All the other chocolate makers followed suit.

In the 20th century, the major chocolate firms began to join forces. In 1904, Kohler became associated with Peter. Nestlé also sought to start manufacturing chocolate and finally, in 1911, it was the turn of Alexandre Cailler (grandson of the company founder), to join them. At that time, the association was called The Swiss Chocolate Society, today it is simply called Nestlé. The company still carefully keeps the recipes developed by Kohler, Cailler and Peter, and in particular those for the preparation of Cailler milk chocolate, Crémant and Nestlé milk chocolate. Swiss chocolate also owes much to Philippe Suchard who, in 1901, created the famous Milka milk chocolate. Another Swiss invention is chocolate fondant. If the chocolate we enjoy today is of a fine, smooth and creamy texture, this was not always the case. The chocolate bars of the beginning of the 19th century were crumbly to the touch and tasted grainy, until Rudolph Lindt invented a new treatment process for the cocoa mass called "conching". Through the addition of cocoa butter, the mass became more homogeneous and more "fondant". In 1899, Sprüngli acquired the Lindt company and built a factory close to Zürich. Today the house of Lindt & Sprüngli is the biggest Swiss chocolate maker. To complete the story, it is noteworthy that the praline made its mark on the Swiss tradition; i.e. the cocoa mass with a caramelised sugar, roasted hazelnuts or almonds and vanilla. Every brand developed its own chocolate praline.

→ Alphonse Marie Mucha,
Nestlé: Respectful Homage,
1897. Private collection.

4

Belgian chocolate

The difficulties of chocolate to breakthrough until the 17th century

In 1477, with the death of Charles the Bold, the Netherlands separated from Burgundy and through inheritance became a dependency of the royal house of Spain. The conquest of the New World, the West Indies therefore had repercussions on the Low Countries. This all began with using sugar, which was received in far greater quantities from the plantations in America, and that made it possible to create more desserts and sweets.

As elsewhere, chocolate was introduced into Flanders by the senior officials, the aristocrats and also the clergy. It remained a very expensive item of food for many years. In the 18th century, it still cost fourteen times as much as a loaf of bread! At that time, the price was between 35 and 50 sous per pound (a worker earned 8 sous per day). The oldest trace of chocolate in Belgium dates back to 1635, where it was cited in an invoice of the abbey of Baudeloo in Ghent. The chocolate in question had been purchased in order to offer as a gift. This is still frequently the case today, and has been reinforced even more since Jean Neuhaus created the praline.

Another trace of chocolate in Belgium in the 17th century was in 1663, when Emmanuel Swares de Rinero was granted the exclusive authorisation to manufacture in the Brabant region. In addition, a book appeared in Brussels in 1682, a medical work entitled *Medicina Pharmaceutica*, describing how cocoa and chocolate were used at the court of the Count de Monterey, Governor of the Netherlands. Whereas while the Spanish added chili pepper, long pepper or aniseed, Count de Monterey added sugar, cinnamon, pepper (although not always, so as not to "overheat the liver") and cocoa vanilla. He did not like his chocolate too spicy, preferring a more refined and delicate flavour.

In 1697, the Flie family of Antwerp purchased a chocolate service of 12 cups and 12 saucers costing 6 francs. This was for private use, and with good reason, since in 1698, the chronicler H. Conincks wrote: "A café has been opened in Mechelen by a Dutchman who arrived here and was living in a house close to the Saint-Rombaud tower; however, after two years, he was obliged to close his commerce because the local people did not have the custom of drinking chocolate, coffee or tea in public establishments, but rather to take their breakfast with a small glass of beer or,

↓ Tasting tea, coffee or chocolate, Delft faïence, *circa* 1710. National Ceramic Museum, Sèvres.

emulating the custom of the workers, with a small glass of distilled anisette with sugar which is good for the health...". And in the following year, 1699, a Royal Edict was issued in the town of Antwerp covering the prohibition of operating cafés or having a coffee, tea or chocolate service, as well as gambling, with a fine of 500 florins and 5 years exile!

The first golden age in the 18th century

In the National Archives in Brussels, and notably in the archives referring to Charles Alexander of Lorraine (1712-1780), there is ample documentation showing considerable consumption of chocolate. From 1744 until his death, the Governor General of the Austrian Netherlands was an undisputed lover of chocolate, without there being any real explanation for this passion. He had probably been influenced by the general infatuation with chocolate that existed in the country. He drank chocolate every morning with breakfast accompanied by bread or biscuits. Other documents exist in archives relating to the court as well as in the papers of noble families and religious establishments. Here are some examples: the Brabant parish priest De Coninck (1755) had a copper chocolate pot, as did the Sint-Niklaasberg convent at Aarschot, where it was placed in the infirmary; the d'Ursel family noted the purchase of tea, coffee and chocolate in their household accounts. Two contemporary reports make mention of chocolate. The first one is *Le Journal de Gisbert Cuper, député en campagne, tenu en Flandres en 1706 (The journal of Gisbert Cuper, envoy, written in Flanders in 1706)* in which he describes drinking chocolate when he visited various notable citizens. The second is dated 1735 and is entitled *Amusemens* (sic) *des eaux de Spa (Amusement when taking the waters at Spa)*. There is a description here of how the dinner guests added a little opium to the chocolate beverage served after the meal in order to be rid of an irritating guest. They neutralised an unwanted guest who was then unable to attend the ball that followed the dinner.

↑ Adam style silver chocolate pot, 1773-1774. Victoria & Albert Museum, London.

An Antwerp chronicle described how the River Scheldt froze during the very harsh winter of 1717 and various stalls were installed on the river where coffee, chocolate, wine and beer were served.

To conclude, in the General Archives of the Kingdom (Saint Hubert records) there are indications that on two occasions, in 1717 and 1764, the monks of the Abbey of Saint Hubert purchased chocolate.

In the chocolate trade, Flanders had the Netherlands as its privileged partner. There is even documentation stating that the Dutch smuggled cocoa coming from Venezuela via Curaçao destined for their home ports, in particular Amsterdam, from where it was sent to Antwerp, Leuven, Nieuwpoort, Ostend and Bruges. In 1741, in a work published in Amsterdam, Jean-Jacques Woyt (a doctor from Copenhagen, Denmark) set down his recommendations as to where the best quality cocoa beans could be purchased: "The beans should be fresh and weighty; they should come from Caraquen beans, the biggest ones, black on the outside and dark red inside, just like roasted almonds; these beans are used to make the well known chocolate; the oil extracted from it is used for the base. The word Caraquen or Caraque is the origin of the Belgian French word "caraque".

To grind the beams, a heated mortar or a chocolate stone was used; it was often a marble stone to avoid dust being mixed with the powder. Before the machine was invented, the workers had to be on their knees to grind the beans. In 1723, the work surface was invented which enabled this hard work to be done while standing. In 1776, a type of compressor roller was activated by hydraulic energy. Later it would be activated by a windmill, by a horse and finally, in 1819, by steam.

↓ Encyclopaedia plates illustrating the craft of the confectioner, 1751-1772. Barry-Callebaut, Chocolate Museum Eupen.

Confiseur, Etuve Four.

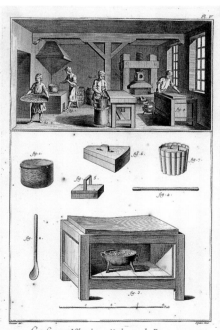

Confiseur, Chocolat et Moules pour les Fromages.

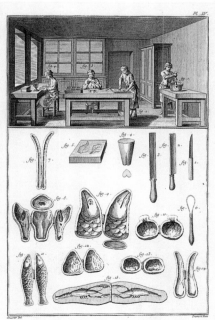

Confiseur, Pastillage et Moulles pour les Glaces.

After adding spices, it was transformed into a mass, placed in a tin or broken into small pieces to make chocolate pastilles, or in cylinder-like rollers. To prepare the beverage, this mass was placed in a cask, water was poured over it and it was then boiled until the chocolate melted. Sugar was added and water until the formation of a fatty froth, which was then drunk. At that time, the best chocolate was made in Turin and Bayonne; in Belgium it was produced by artisans.

The recipes were numerous and varied. One of the most delicate ones proposed a mixture of chocolate, cinnamon, sugar, eggs, honey, orange blossom and amber! Flemish cookery books of the 18th century featured chocolate as a flavouring agent. There was a recipe for a "chocolate pie" in *Le Chef Parfait (The Perfect chef)* a cookery book from the Abbey of Afflighem, near Alost, Belgium. It dates from the same century. "Take two spoonfuls of wheat flour and place in a saucepan, take 6 egg yolks, beat the egg whites until stiff and set aside, add yolks to the flour and one pint of sweet milk well beaten, add ¼ oz. of crushed chocolate, cinnamon, sugar, grated zest of lemon, mix well together and bring to the boil, allow to cool and when the mixture is cold, add the stiff egg whites, mix well again, then place the mixture into a pre-cooked flaky pastry pie-crust, sprinkle with sugar, coat with beaten egg yolks and bake in the oven until golden brown; serve hot or cold."

→ Shop sign of a chocolate maker. Museum of Milan, Milan.

The first chocolate services

↑ Silver chocolate pot, 1686.
Château de Laarne.

↑ Neuhaus chocolate pot in
china. Neuhaus Collection.

→ Silver chocolate pot,
circa 1900. Museum of
Decorative Arts, Paris.

The manufacturing plant in the southern region of the Netherlands in the 18th century were mainly located in Antwerp, Mons, Bruges, Liège, Brussels, Mechelen and Tournai. Chocolate pots were made there. The most usual form was a pear shape, mounted on three or four little legs. The chocolate pot was made of silver, porcelain, pewter, tin or terra cotta. The handle was in wood or ivory. At the beginning of the century, the Compagnie Ostendaise sent plans and designs for porcelain decoration to China. The Tournai porcelain factory was founded in 1750 and mass produced cups, with or without handles, with or without saucers. The chocolate service was more expensive than the tea or coffee service.

Naturally, the chocolate pot resembled a coffee pot. The great difference was in the hole in the lid. The purpose of the hole was to be able to introduce the whisk without lifting the lid and thereby cooling the chocolate, this rod was used to make the liquid frothy. The hole could be sealed with a small cap that could be unscrewed or simply lifted.

The chocolate pot was such a luxury item that, for example, it was awarded as the first prize presented by Charles Alexander of Lorraine at the end of the academic year at the Antwerp Academy. Thus, the young sculptor Joseph Gillis (1724-1773) received one bearing the ducal coat of arms and Latin inscriptions for the 1750 examinations.

It is clear that there was an abundance of chocolate services and chocolate pots in the dressers of the nobility, the bourgeoisie and the clergy in the region that was to become Belgium. It was a way of displaying luxury and power, since coffee and tea services had become more widespread and classless. Showing outsiders that the family drank chocolate was an indication of a high social level. Even if the family did not actually drink chocolate, as can be seen from the example of the Marquis de Herzelles, President of the Council of Finances, in 1740 and Count de Lalaing, who drank neither tea nor chocolate, and only rarely coffee! Fernand Braudel records in his book *Civilisation and Capitalism* (1967): "Those in high places occasionally drank chocolate, the elderly often, and the lower classes never."

Chocolate manufacturing is growing in Belgium.
However, it is one of those industries that do not
present a particular advantage for the country,
given that few workers are required and
the raw materials come partly from abroad.

(The Exhibition of Belgian Industry jury, 1847)

→ Jean Neuhaus, fourth from
the right and Pierre De Gavre,
second on the right, in the
confectionery workshop.

The industrial era of Belgian chocolate

↑ Chocolat Rubis iron chocolate box, Verviers. Barry-Callebaut, Chocolate Museum, Eupen.

↓ Hardy's iron box for desert chocolate, Verviers. Barry-Callebaut, Chocolate Museum, Eupen.

The first steam-driven machine in the chocolate industry in Belgium was installed in Brussels in 1835; it was the only one until 1850. It was a lightweight, two-horse-power machine for grinding the roasted cocoa beans. At that time, there were thirty-odd chocolate makers in Brussels. Among them were "La Veuve Claret", a manufacturer of fine and hygienic chocolates, "Cordier" (Confectioner to the King) and "'t Sander" (confectioner and chocolate maker). Just as today, Easter and December were the most profitable periods for chocolate makers who had to produce something different from the rest of the year, hence all the special patisserie and confectionery. In the mid-19th century, chocolate makers were represented mostly by artisan workshops with just one worker. In the period 1840-1850, chocolate exports to the Netherlands, Luxemburg and Prussia reached 500 kg per year. The Exhibition of Belgian Industry was held in 1847 and the jury did not award any prizes to the only chocolate maker who exhibited, Berwaerts of Brussels. The jury declared, "Chocolate manufacturing is growing in Belgium. However, it is one of those industries that do not present a particular advantage for the country, given that few workers are required and the raw materials come partly from abroad."

Nevertheless, from 1860 onwards, the industry's development was rapid and inexorable: one new steam-activated machine was installed every year. In 20 years, the number of chocolate manufacturers had doubled. Consumer demand had grown alongside a growing and prosperous economy supported by financiers, enterprises, and also the bourgeoisie enriched by trade and property. People were eating in restaurants and parties were organised in private homes. Chocolate was still associated with a luxurious style of living.

The most flagrant fraud at the time was the partial replacement of the ingredients of cocoa by poor quality fats. To combat this deception, Belgian chocolate was patented in 1884. It was prohibited to sell, transport, or possess a product bearing the name "chocolate" unless it contained at least 35% pure cocoa. (This was to be a problem when the neighbouring countries were allowing 32%!)

By the end of the 19th century, Belgium had 63 chocolate producing enterprises. Decentralisation was in vogue. Four companies stayed in Brussels (including, of

course, Neuhaus who had been there since 1857, and Senez-Strubelle), the other companies moved to the suburbs: Anderlecht, Ixelles, Schaerbeek (Côte d'Or), Molenbeek, Laeken (Meyers-Courtois) welcomed 11 manufacturers. In the provinces, the artisans' workshops were gradually converted into factories: Martougin, Baron and Meurisse in Antwerp, Cacao Goemaere in Ghent, Bocquet, Delannoy and Joveneau in Tournai, Jacques in Verviers, and Kwatta in Bois-d'Haine. In 1887, the Union of master pastry cooks founded their own chocolate factory.

In the trade directory of 1891, a one-pound packet of imported chocolate, categorised as "good ordinary quality" cost BEF 2.50 (a bricklayer's wage for 10 hours work), whereas the most expensive packet of chocolate cost BEF 5.50.

During the 19th century, many patents were registered for the innovations developed in the chocolate industry. For example, a "digestive chocolate powder" in 1866, a "chocolate-flavoured gingerbread" in 1871, as well as a "tapping table" proposed by Joveneau of Tournai in 1879, an "apparatus for crumbling chocolate" in 1884 and a "tablet cutting device" in 1885.

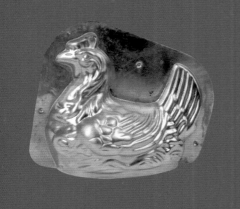
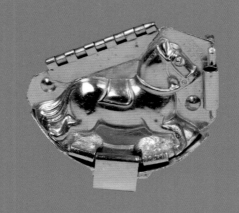
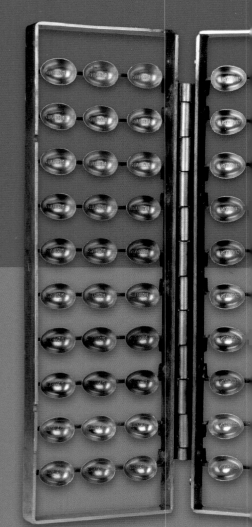
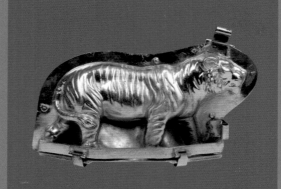

Belgian mould makers

Production of finely worked chocolate moulds started in 1832. It followed the fashion, history and culture of society in its choice of subjects: tasty, three-dimensional images that are pleasing to see, and agreeable to the touch. A fun way for children to learn! When the motor driven grinder replaced the hand kneading of the cocoa mass, the chocolate makers could let their fantasy take flight in shape design. Jean-Baptiste Létang, a Breton, founded the first workshop for producing chocolate moulds in Paris in 1832. Apart from silver and pewter, the mould makers also worked in copper and iron, which are malleable and good heat conductors. Scrap tin-plate and tin were then replaced by nickel plated metal which is more resistant to wear. Then stainless steel was used, which prevented the chocolate from sticking to the mould, and plastic with its unbeatable prices.

Traces have been found in Brussels of E. et Ch. Dunan (1888-1929), a company specialising in metal moulds and later the firms Cupri (1922), Lavallé (1925). The Metro company of Deurne manufactured moulds between 1945 and 1966. Bakelite, the first synthetic resin, invented in 1906 by a Ghent chemist living in the United States, Léo Hendrik Baekeland, was used by the Marco company of St Niklaas (1947-1975). Finally, at Sint-Pieters-Leeuw, Belmoplast (1949-1965) produced chocolate moulds in plastic.

As for the choice of subjects, in addition to animals and the usual objects, there were St Nicholas, Father Christmas, the Gilles de Binche, Manneken Pis and Tintin. The Royals were often represented, and all kinds of transport modes that thrilled the children: motorbikes, automobiles, aeroplanes and rockets.

← Chocolate moulds. Neuhaus collection.

A new golden age for Belgian chocolate

→ Côte d'Or chocolate factory.
La Fonderie, Brussels.

The 20th century saw the consecration of Belgium as "the land of chocolate". At the beginning of the century, there were about 50 chocolate makers in Belgium. Visionary entrepreneurs such as Alfred Martougin leapt into the great chocolate adventure. He was a Walloon who created a model chocolate factory in Antwerp in 1902, and his name has remained linked to the international renown of Belgian chocolate. In 1909, the Bruyerre chocolate factory was established in Charleroi, named after its founder Léon-François Bruyerre; in 1911, Callebaut added a chocolate department to its factory in Wieze, started in 1850; Mary Delluc opened a chocolate boutique called 'Mary' on the Rue Royale in 1919, the same year that August Verheecke opened a patisserie near Bruges that was to become the Kathy company; in 1920 Léonidas Kestelidès, a member of the Greek delegation from the United States attending the Brussels Universal Exhibition, fell in love with a young lady from Brussels, they married and launched the Léonidas chocolate brand in Ghent; Joseph Libeerts created the Italo-Suisse company at Izegem and Roulers in 1923.

The report entitled *Exposé de la situation du Royaume (Review of the situation of the Kingdom)*, included the comment: "several years ago, chocolate was still considered to be a luxury item; it has now become an article that consumers purchase as a matter of course." The decrease in the price of chocolate (particularly due to lower sugar prices and a reduction in the price of cocoa beans) – almost 80% over a few years – had helped to win the hearts, not only of the entire Belgian population, but also of buyers in foreign markets. Before the 1914-1918 war, the working class was also in the habit of consuming chocolate, it was not reserved solely for the better off members of society.

Chocolate always makes people dreamy, especially children who receive chocolates for the celebration of Saint Nicolas and Christmas. In his novel *Het leven van Rozeken van Dalen*, Cyriel Buysse describes a wedding banquet in a Flemish village where the guests are drinking hot chocolate; in 1907, Stijn Streuvels described poor schoolchildren staring into a shop full of sweets and chocolates.

At the beginning of the century in Brussels, the public transport company proposed closed carriages for the tramways: "Painted in brown with the lower part and

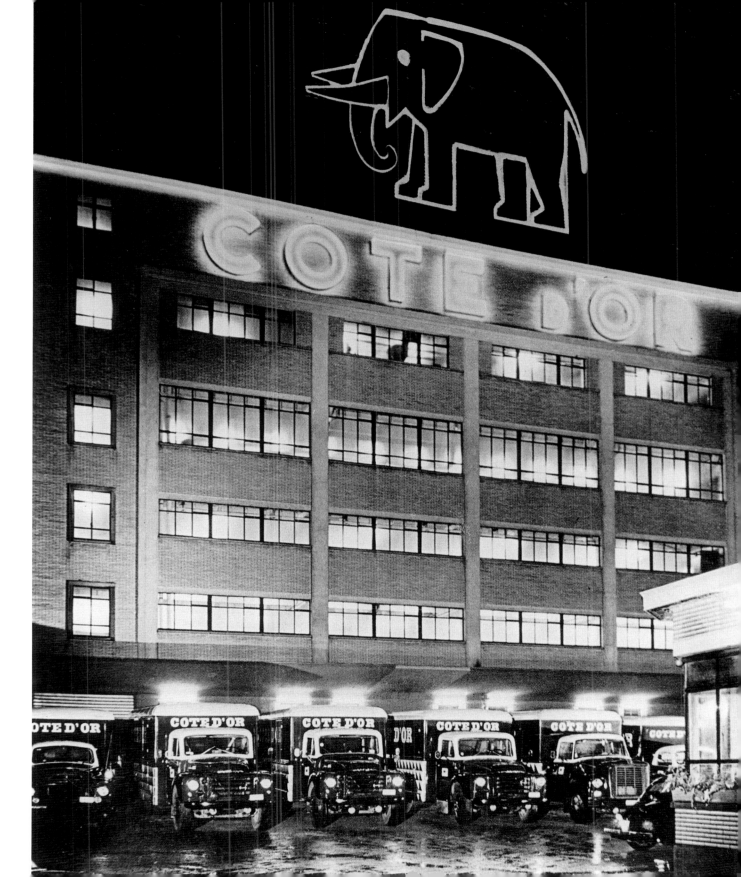

CHOCOLATERIE CALLEBAUT WIEZE
UNE VUE DE NOS USINES OÙ L'ON FABRIQUE LE MEILLEUR DES CHOCOLATS
EEN ZICHT ONZER FABRIEK WAAR DE ALLERFIJNSTE CHOCOLADE BEREID WORDT.

E. HEUVELMANS, GAND

→ Callebaut chocolate factory
at Wieze. Barry-Callebaut
collection, Lebbeke-Wieze.

under structure a creamy white, the "Economy" carriages were soon called 'chocolate trams'. The regulars said "Chocolat!" to the driver and he knew they wanted a connecting ticket for another tram, according to History of public transport in Brussels (in French). In 1913, public transport vehicles in Brussels were all painted primrose yellow.

After the war, people continued to eat chocolate, but rather than just having it for parties and celebrations, it became a Belgian habit to eat chocolate virtually every day. It was not just due to the prestigious image of chocolate, but also its great energy value. A. Boden, of the Belgian chocolate industry's professional body explained at the 1930 congress, "if we consider the nutritional value of chocolate, it costs less than other food items." In addition, there are other advantages: a bar of chocolate can be eaten quickly and it is a good appetite suppressant. More and more places started to sell chocolate: grocers, newsagents... and then co-op stores, hypermarkets and supermarkets, vending machines and retail chains which often sold their own brands of chocolate.

Advertising also encouraged the increased consumption of chocolate. Even at that time, the message was "Great Belgian chocolate!" Its massive distribution followed the law of supply and demand between 1945 and 1980, making chocolate a new of item of daily consumption.

Belgian inventions

In addition to the fabulous inventions of the praline and the 'ballotin' by Neuhaus, Belgians have been responsible for other innovations. The chocolate bar, that is called "bâton" in Belgium, was created by Kwatta in 1921. The company launched small 30 g and 45 g bars of chocolate. The other manufactures followed suit very rapidly. It is noteworthy that it is particularly in Belgium that the chocolate bar has proved a huge success, elsewhere it is luxury item that is relatively expensive compared with buying a tablet. The first "filled bâton" was launched in 1936 by the firm Jacques, which had already been offering chromos since 1905, but found another outlet here. This should not be confused with the 'candy-bar', the 'snack', which represents a 30% market share, and contains malt extracts, puffed rice bubbles, etc. Chocolate spread was also invented in Belgium. Côte d'Or proposed the spread under the name of Pastador in 1952.

Another invention revolutionised the manufacture of chocolate: transporting chocolate in liquid form. Charles Callebaut, a major supplier of "cover chocolate" (bulk supply), was responsible for this turnaround in the process. Tank trucks of 10 or 20 tonnes delivered liquid chocolate, kept at approximately 35ºC, to three-quarters of the clients. Using this delivery method, two phases become redundant: the refrigeration phase and the reheating phase for working the chocolate; thus the chocolate obviously retains more flavour and aroma. Moreover, the refrigeration machines consumed a considerable amount of energy and, when transporting chocolate in liquid form, the calorific value of the trucks and engines is recuperated.

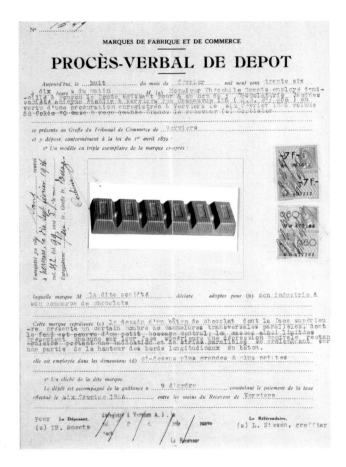

↑ Jacques chocolate, registration document for the registration of a chocolate bar, dated 8 February 1936. "This brand represents the design of a chocolate bar with the upper surface presenting a certain number of transversal flutings, etc."

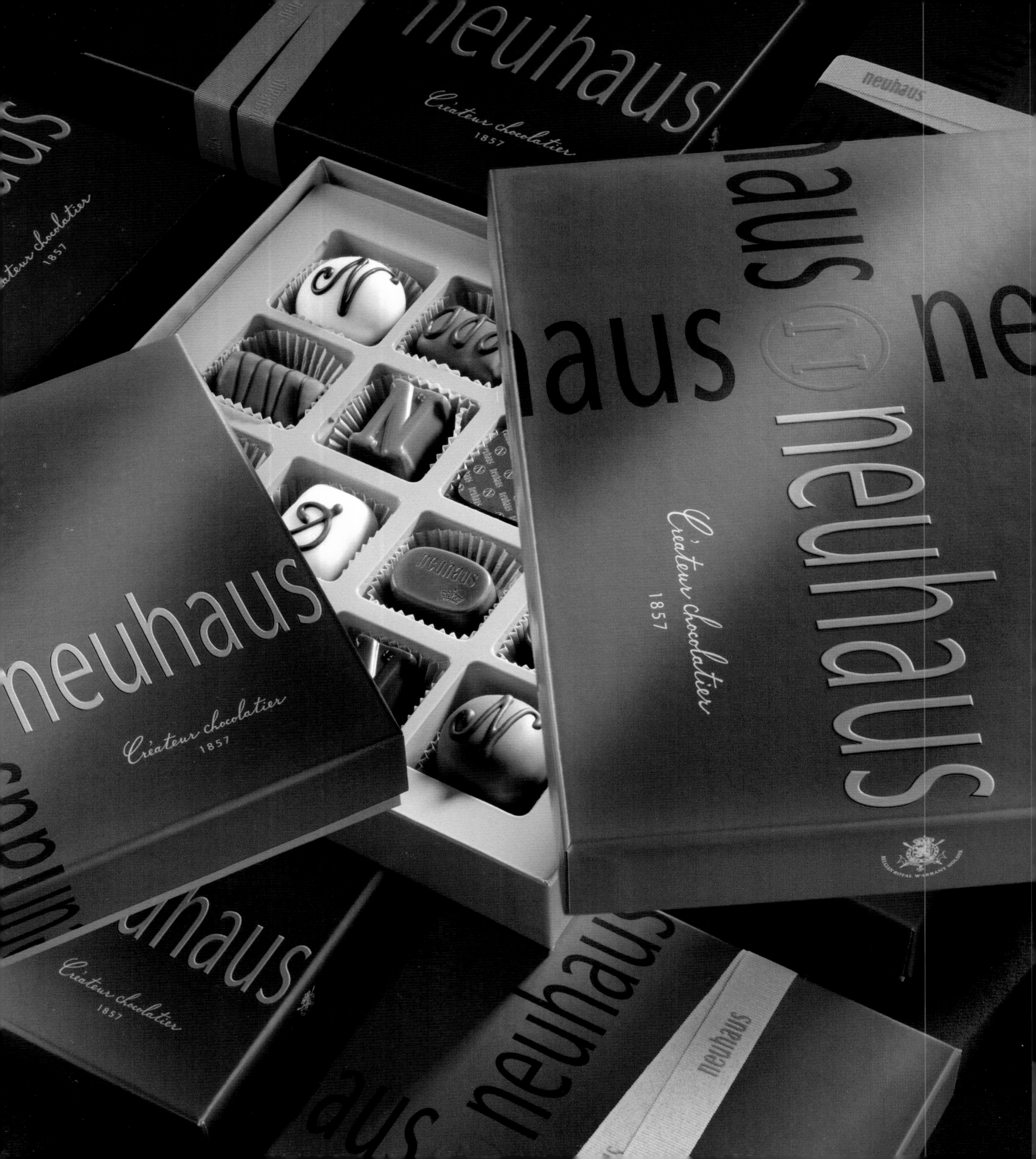
neuhaus
Créateur chocolatier
1857

Belgium in the lead!

Belgian chocolate is the best chocolate in the world. Five reasons are often cited to corroborate this statement. The first is the quality of the cocoa bean used in Belgium. Great care is always taken when choosing the beans. Most of the time, buyers visit the plantations to survey the harvest, sometimes even buying directly from the growers. The second reason is the particular care taken in the roasting and grinding. Whereas in the United Kingdom, for example, for reasons of time and money, the grinding is carried out to 24 microns, in Belgium the grinding goes down to 12 microns. There is no doubt that the aroma is more intense. Reason number three is the quality of the other ingredients: particularly the sugar, which is also produced in Belgium. The fourth reason is the percentage of cocoa. The minimum legal percentage allowed for a product to carry the name 'chocolate' is 35%; it is not unusual to find up to 43% on average. The fifth and last reason is the know-how and obvious passion of all the chocolate makers, from the most modest artisan to the senior executive of a multinational organisation. These qualities of the chocolate, enhanced by the fact that traditionally and historically it is a favourite of the Belgian consumer, make Belgium the world's leader in high quality chocolate production.

The Belgians are the world's biggest consumers of chocolate. In Belgium, 5.8 kg of chocolate are consumed per year per inhabitant, followed by Iceland (5.1 kg), Luxemburg and Ireland (4.7 kg), Switzerland (4.5 kg), France (3.8 kg), Norway (3.7 kg), United Kingdom (3.6 kg), Germany (3.5 kg), and Denmark (2.9 kg). These statistics relate to ground cocoa beans and net imports of cocoa derivative products, chocolate and chocolate-based products issued by the ICCO (International Cocoa Organisation).

Chocolate's place in History

The Jesuits and chocolate

The Jesuits were the most successful evangelists in the New World. They adopted local customs, including drinking chocolate. For a certain period, they even held the monopoly of the trading and distribution of cocoa beans. For the Jesuits, this was a way of enhancing their appeal to the natives. They clashed with the Dominicans and Franciscans on this issue. There was even a distinction between northern Europe, viewed as austere coffee drinkers and southern Europe, perceived as lascivious chocolate drinkers! It is true that chocolate's reputation as an aphrodisiac was more present than ever. In the 17th century, the church had to pronounce on the nutritional nature of chocolate: in other words, could one consume it during Lent? It was a 'liquid', it could be drunk during the period of fasting (*Liquidum non frangiat jejunum*), if it was considered a 'solid food', given the consistency of the mass, it was prohibited. Much argumentation took place. In 1591, a Spanish doctor living in the New World, Juan de Cardenas, took a position by considering it as a food item likely to break the abstinence. Yet, several years later in 1644, Antonio de Escobar y Mendoza (1589-1669) a Spanish churchman, famous preacher and voluminous writer, wrote: "Simple chocolate is a beverage that cannot be considered as breaking the fast". The discussions ended in 1664 when Cardinal Francesco Maria Brancaccion took the position in favour of chocolate: Even though chocolate is not primarily a food item, it can be that it proves nourishing, by accident. In conclusion, he wrote that chocolate should be considered as a liquid, just as wine or beer. A decree issued by the Holy Office in 1666 ended the discussion by restricting the consumption of chocolate during Lent to a strict minimum and only when mixed with water; sugar and milk not being allowed during the fasting period.

← Charles Joseph Natoire, *Louise-Anne de Bourbon dressed as an imaginary monk holding the cord of St. Francis*, 18th century. Versailles Palace and Trianon Palace, Versailles.

↓ Antonio de Léon Pinelo, *There is a moral issue regarding whether drinking chocolate breaks the ecclesiastical fast*, Madrid, 1636. National Library of France, Paris.

No sooner have you swallowed a generous mouthful

This pearl, this jewel, this marvellous potion of the Americas

It has barely begun to melt within you

Yet it cleanses you and purifies you

of all bitterness and all mortal cares.

Seeping into your arteries and your veins

in a beauteous concoction of vermilion sauce,

By its pleasant and free flow, it recalls

The torrid heat of the sun.

(Henry Stubbes, 1662)

A beverage for the depraved

Madame de Sévigné, initially enthusiastic about chocolate, concluded by finding it had a diabolical nature. Here is an extract from a letter of 1671: "Chocolate is flattering for a while, then it brings on a continuous fever that brings you to death's door... The Marquise de Coëtlogon consumed so much chocolate that, being with child, she gave birth to a little boy who was as black as the devil".

Chocolate was always surrounded by myths and the imaginary, which made it an "Indian nectar". The English poet Henry Stubbes wrote a poem dedicated to chocolate in 1662: *No sooner have you swallowed a generous mouthful / This pearl, this jewel, this marvellous potion of the Americas / It has barely begun to melt within you / Yet it cleanses you and purifies you / of all bitterness and all mortal cares. / Seeping into your arteries and your veins / in a beauteous concoction of vermilion sauce, / By its pleasant and free flow, it recalls / The torrid heat of the sun.*

In the *Traité des aliments (A Treatise on foodstuffs)*, published in 1702, the author, Louis Lémery states that chocolate has aphrodisiac properties that are stimulating. Chocolate can therefore be added to the list of European aphrodisiac foods: game, caviar, truffles, spices, etc. Even though the ambiance when one is indulging in such foods and the gallant partner with whom one is sharing them must surely have a strong influence, it cannot be denied that these foods arouse desire. Moreover, a 17th century Viennese doctor, Johann Michael Haider described chocolate then as "Veneris pabulum" (the food of Venus).

In his memoirs, Marshal de Belle-Isle wrote of the levée of the Regent Philippe II, Duke of Orléans (1674-1723): "The Regent did not have a little levée because this Prince, less discreet than decent, did not want to reveal to the avid and malicious gaze of his courtiers, the presence of dancers from the Opéra in a state of undress, and supposedly decent women in like condition. After he got up, His Royal Highness used to take his chocolate in a large salon where his courtiers came to pay him court."

Among the ardent enthusiasts of chocolate in the 18th century, there was Madame du Barry (1743-1793), the favourite of Louis XV, who gave frothy chocolate to her lovers; Casanova, Chevalier de Seingalt (1725-1798), noted in his *Histoire de ma vie*

→ Thomas Rowlandson,
The chocolate house, 1787.
Museum of London,
London.

(The history of my life) which he wrote in French: "one can restore one's vigour by eating boiled meat balls made of *béatilles* (an old term meaning a pie made from sweetmeats, foie gras and mushrooms) and of course, frothy chocolate"; the Marquise de Pompadour (1721-1764), another favourite of Louis XV, regularly drank decilitres of chocolate with amber to arouse her desire, according to the memoirs of Madame du Hausset.

The case of the divine Marquis, Donatien Alphonse François de Sade (1740-1814) is rather particular. He led a debauched life and sometimes used chocolate as a means to an evil end. He offered chocolate pastilles to all the ladies invited to his ball held in Marseille. However, he had filled them with cantharidine, a powerful congestant alkaloid extracted from an insect from the South of France. He admitted it in court, where he was summoned several days later following a formal complaint from a husband... Sade wrote in *The 120 days of Sodom*: "At eleven o'clock, we went to the women's apartment where the eight young Sultanas appeared before us naked and served chocolate to us."

Chocolate as medication

Originally, when chocolate was being introduced into Europe, it was presented as a medication. The Indians ascribed properties to it: an aphrodisiac, as has been seen, but also invigorating and nutritional. Jean-Frédéric Cartheuser, a German doctor and chemist declared, "Chocolate is very beneficial for people who are thin, convalescing from a long illness, who have been feeling languid or have experienced major blood loss…"

Alphonse de Richelieu, archbishop of Lyon, the elder brother of the famous Cardinal de Richelieu, seems to have been the first person to have really used chocolate as medication. He used cocoa "to modify the vapours of the spleen". Alphonse de Richelieu claimed to be the repository of the secret of the Spanish monks.

← Henri Georges Bréard,
The cup of chocolate – circa 1912.
Location unknown.

In general, other ingredients were added to chocolate to help with healing or soothing illness. For example, the apothecaries of the period added cinnamon to chocolate to relieve the kidneys, achiota to help with breathing, rhubarb to reduce bile, and ambergris to strengthen the heart.

One recipe that has been kept is "chocolate à la capucine" named for a Capuchin from Martinique; this was supposed to enable you to spend the whole day without eating, except for the evening meal: "Put in a bowl and mix well: 4 oz. chocolate, 6 oz. sugar, 3 eggs beaten well with a good half-litre Madeira!"

From the 16th century onwards, people applied chocolate to their skin to relieve chest colds and make the muscles supple.

↑ Albert Anker, *The cup of chocolate – circa* 1867. Bethnal Green Museum, London.

During the next century, several theses were presented at the faculty of medicine in Paris supporting the argument of the salubriousness of chocolate, with enthusiastic conclusions. The medical profession in the 17th and 18th centuries acknowledged a broad range of therapeutic actions. Its nutritional value was judged to be greater than that of meat.

Louis Lémery summarised the situation by stating that chocolate is a tonic, that it aids the digestion and softens pungent humours, it is an aphrodisiac and stimulates conception. It is a stimulant and strengthens the memory.

A British doctor, Henry Mundy, told this story: "I once knew a man who was consumptive and in a virtually desperate state; he sought refuge by drinking chocolate. To please him, his wife did the same, and this had the effect of a double miracle. The man was soon back on his feet and his wife, who had previously been considered barren, became pregnant by her husband and gave birth to triplets, three viable babies."

Four chocolates which are good for your health

In 1849, a society of members of the Institute and Academy of Medicine in Paris published a comprehensive survey with the long title: *Dictionnaire de Médecine actuelle à l'usage des gens du monde, des chefs de famille et des grands établissements, des administrateurs, des magistrats et des officiers de police judiciaire, enfin pouvant servir de direction à tous ceux qui se dévouent au soulagement des malades (Dictionary of contemporary medicine addressed to worldly readers, heads of families and large establishments, administrators, magistrates and officers of the police force, to serve as guidelines to all those who are involved in relieving the conditions of the sick)!* The author of the chapter on chocolate, a certain Clisson, describes the discovery and manufacture of chocolate, but he also goes into detail about four types of choc-

↓ Advertisement for Kassel chocolate, 1908. Library of Decorative Arts, Paris.

olate and their health properties. Simple chocolate cannot be categorised as a health product since it only contains cocoa beans and sugar. It is heavy on the stomach and has a low nutritional value. Chocolate flavoured with vanilla, amber or cinnamon, has a better taste and is easily digested. These additional aromatic substances have the effect of "slight stimulation on the digestive system, are pleasing to the senses and aid digestion, as well as pleasant to taste and smell. The best way to absorb it in this case is mixed with water and not with milk." Starchy or analeptic chocolate contains substances such as sago, tapioca, arrow-root, or salep. The text continues: "It is one of the best foods for people who are weak, thin, or delicate, and it is good for women, children and the elderly, convalescents and anyone who is of a nervous disposition or has a poor appetite. It will stimulate and support their strength, improve the level of activity of all their bodily functions and help them to put on weight. In our society,

HAUSEN's KASSELER HAFER-KAKAO

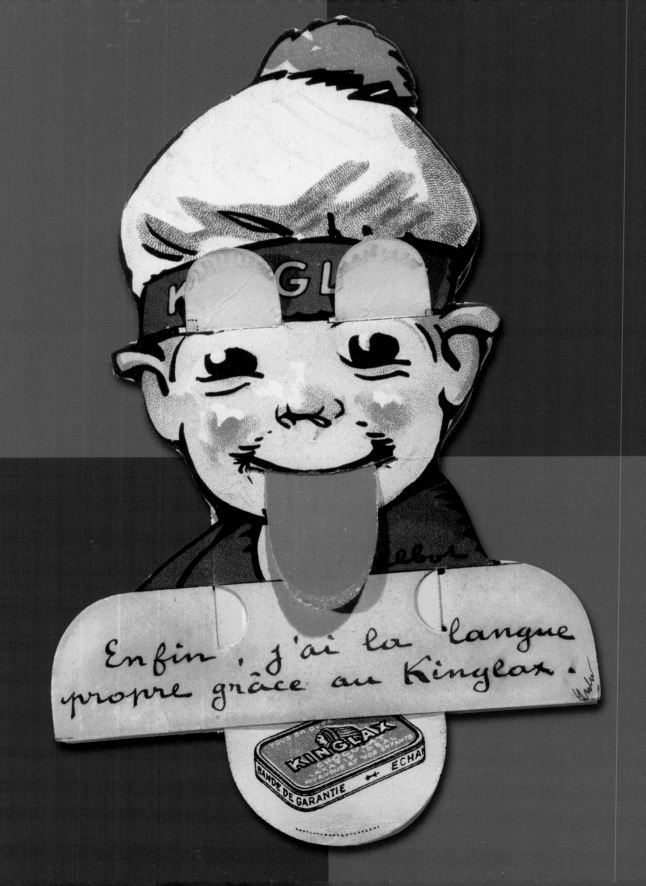

it is thought to cause constipation; this is yet another of the one thousand and one errors that are attributed to the general public and which we attempt to put right, often in vain." Finally, Clisson reports on the fourth chocolate: the pharmacodynamic, medicinal chocolate. "This chocolate provides a rather good method of disguising the bitter, pungent, salty or sharp taste of many drugs that patients find veritably repugnant, yet they willingly take the medication without noticing any bad taste whatsoever when mixed with the chocolate."

The author provides an impressive list: "For the chocolate designed as a tonic and for stomach pains, etc., the simple cocoa mass is mixed with a little extract of cinchona, quassia, colombo, gentian, small centaury, menyanthe, hops, knapweed, germander, and bugleweed; for the chocolate designed for chest infections, Iceland lichen and various starches are added; for the purgative chocolate, scammony, *aloïs*, Jalap, and rhubarb; for the anthelmintic chocolate, add *sémentine*, Corsican corraline algae, ferns, etc.; for the chocolate reputed to be an aphrodisiac, add amber, musk, chives, etc." The author concludes the article by warning people against a deception that chocolates are antisyphilitic and homeopathic!

In the 19th century, there was still the notion in medicine of treating the "humours" and doctors recommended or prohibited chocolate depending on whether the patient was "bilious" or "pituitous". Obviously partly due to chemistry and the possibilities of medical analysis, as well as the rationalising effect of experiments, modern medicine was born in the latter half of the 20th century and its approach to chocolate was different.

← Francisque Poulbot, advertisement for Kinglax laxative chocolate, beginning of 20th century. Private collection.

↓ Poster for Baker & Co. homeopathic chocolate, 19th century. Private collection.

Medicine today

Today, the scientists have decrypted what chocolate can offer and what it does not offer and it is clear that the terms 'medication' and 'aphrodisiac' have been over-appropriated! Chocolate is a high energy food because it contains many carbohydrates and lipids: 500 kcal per 100 grams (550 kcal in milk chocolate). 100 grams of dark chocolate can provide one-quarter of the average daily needs of a woman which are in the region of 1,800 to 2,000 kcal/day. Chocolate contains about one hundred antioxidant chemical substances (flavonoids, of the polyphenol family or "tannins") which have been discovered in the cocoa bean and they are the source of its qualities. These substances possess many virtues: theobromine (an alkaloid psychostimulant that stimulates muscle performance, accelerates the nervous influx, and reduces the effects of stress by blocking the adrenalin receptors) and caffeine have an energizing effect, both increase the secretion of epinephrine, a hormone that is akin to adrenalin.

Four squares of chocolate contain as much caffeine as an espresso. The aphrodisiac effect is produced by phenylethylamine (PEA), 0.4-0.6 micrograms per gram of chocolate. This molecule stimulates the brain to produce dopamine. Chocolate also has an anti-ageing effect thanks to vitamin E and particularly the flavonoids which are antioxidants and neutralise the free radicals (just like fruit and vegetables). The flavonoids are good for the heart too. Chocolate, moreover, is a muscle relaxant because it is rich in magnesium. In general terms, chocolate is also rich in phosphorus, potassium and iron. 100 grams of chocolate can provide one-third of our daily mineral needs. Chocolate has neither a positive nor

Bébé, un peu éprouvé par les premières chaleurs, ne prend plus avec plaisir que sa « PAPILLA MEXICAINE »

CHOCOLAT MEXICAIN, PEU SUCRÉ, LE PLUS DIGESTIF

negative effect on the bad type of cholesterol. Cocoa butter is in fact made up of equal parts of saturated fatty acids, which facilitate the formation of the 'bad' cholesterol and unsaturated fatty acids which encourage the formation of the 'good' cholesterol. Chocolate also contains an endogenous molecule: anandamide. The effects of this molecule could be compared with those of cannabis, which explains the euphoria inducing effects of chocolate. However, this molecule is only present in minuscule quantities. Anandamide generates a removal of the inhibition of dopamine production, thereby increasing indirectly the amount of dopamine produced.

In 2006, researchers from Harvard and Boston discovered that consuming chocolate improved the function of blood vessels. Flavanols, a natural ingredient of the cocoa bean, are responsible for this improvement, which is particularly crucial for the elderly. "This is the first study that demonstrates this fact and the conclusion offers an immense potential that will have an influence on the health of our ageing populations", declared Naomi Fisher, Assistant Professor at the Harvard School of Medicine.

Finally, it is good to repeat some salient truths: chocolate does not lead to liver episodes, it does not cause acne or allergies, it does not trigger migraine headaches, it does not lead to constipation and it does not cause dental caries. Quite the contrary, since a team of scientists from Montpellier CIRAD (centre for international cooperation in agronomical research for development) have just demonstrated that cocoa participates in the prevention of dental caries, thanks to its high fluorine and phosphate content. However, no excesses!

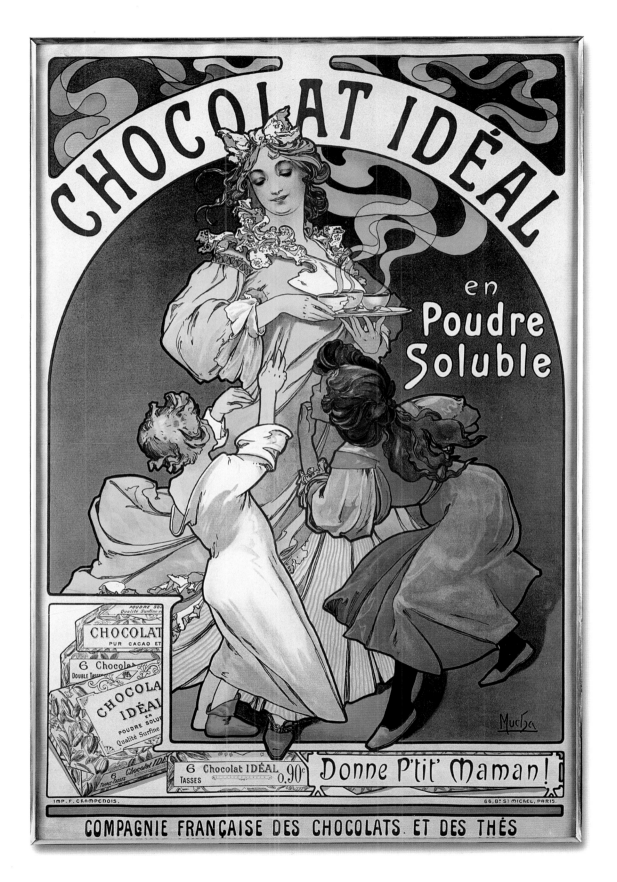

She must have her chocolate every morning,
attentions without end. She constantly
complained of her nerves, her chest and her liver.
The noise of footsteps made her ill; when people left her,
solitude became odious to her; if they came back,
it was doubtless to see her die.

(Gustave Flaubert, *Madame Bovary*,1857)

The effect of chocolate on the brain

It has been proven that chocolate has an effect on the cerebral regions of the brain concerned with pleasure. Chocolate stimulates the orbitofrontal cortex, which is the area of the brain linked to the notion of reward, and perhaps this generates feelings of pleasure. Adam Drewnowski, Professor of Epidemiology and Medicine at the University of Washington in Seattle and Director of the Centre for Public Health and Nutrition, has stated: "In reality, the studies carried out by our team like those realised by other research teams demonstrate that chocolate has absolutely no pharmacological properties. Its effects on behaviour are the same as other foodstuffs with a high sugar and fat content. The only physiological response resulting from consuming chocolate that we have observed is the production of endorphins in the brain, but only in women suffering from bulimia in our study and not in our control subjects, exactly as when eating sugar or fats." This means that the only chocoholics are people suffering with bulimia, and what could possibly trigger an addiction is not the cocoa but the ingredients that the chocolate maker adds to the chocolate. It is noteworthy to state that according to doctors, a chocoholic is someone who consumes between 100 grams and 150 grams of chocolate per day.

The chocolate cure

It is well known that chocolate is good for our moods, but it also seems, and the Mayas understood this, that it is good for the skin and hair. Massages with chocolate and honey are offered, with cocoa bean chips being rolled over the skin to remove dead cells. The body can be enveloped in chocolate mousse for slimming and then be massaged with moisturizing vanilla oil.

Hair care involves applying a nettle-based lotion to stimulate the scalp, greasing the hair with a hot butter and dark chocolate cream, perfumed with several drops of essential oils of orange and cinnamon. This should be followed by a steam bath to enhance the effectiveness of the treatment.

With a cocoa pod base, rich in vitamins and minerals, vanilla and ginger, we find an exfoliation cleanser, an energising soap, a nourishing cream and a massage balm. Not only do these products moisturize dry skin but they instil a feeling of wellbeing, it appears. It is said that 74% of clients visiting these 'chocolate cure' centres leave feeling happier after inhaling during ten minutes of cocoatherapy treatment!

A hotel in Pennsylvania, USA, is offering unusual mellow rejuvenation cures. Clients can take bubbling baths mixed with one-eighth of a cup of unsweetened cocoa powder and one-third of a cup of instant skimmed milk powder. In another room lit by chocolate perfumed candles, a client is wrapped in a rich chocolate mud mixed with cocoa essence. Chocolate encourages the blood circulation, while cocoa butter is being used to moisturize tired skin – these are the words used to advertise these cures!

Sensation chocolate massage and exfoliation oil, Paris.

Le Cacao

The baptism of the cocoa bean

Until 1737, botanists had called the cocoa bean "Amygdala pecuniaria" (pecuniary almond) or "Avellana Mexicana" (Mexican almond). However, in that year, the Swedish naturalist Carl von Linné (1707-1778), author of the famous classification of animal and plant species, named the almond "Theobroma cacao" (cacao – beverage of the gods). Perhaps he was inspired by Bachot's declaration at the Faculty of Medicine in Paris 50 years earlier, who stated: "Chocolate is such a noble confection that instead of nectar and ambrosia, it should be called the true food of the gods, and it is more deserving of deification than the mushrooms of Emperor Claudius." This new name became established in Europe at a time when medicine was undergoing a major transformation. At that time, chocolate was primarily considered as medication before being perceived as a delicacy. Also during that period, the natural sciences, and in particular botany, were in a state of complete change. Clusius, the pen name of the botanist Charles De L'escluse (1526-1609), had for example written works devoted to exotic plants in which he described the cocoa bean as follows: "This fruit appears very like an almond removed from its shell; it is covered with a fine black membrane containing the kernel. It has an astringent and unpleasant taste." In the same way, Jean Bauhin (1541-1613), in his *Universal History of Plants*, published in 1651 after his death, wrote in all simplicity: "The cocoa of America or Mexican hazelnut is the fruit of a tree that has the leaves of a chestnut tree and fruit resembling an almond."

Finally, it was the Dominican father Jean-Baptiste Labat (1663-1738) who gave an accurate and detailed observation in his work *New Voyage to the islands of America*. Industrial production obviously led the men of science to become more interested in this tree and its fruit.

← *Cocoa.* Charles Plumier, *Plants from Martinique and Guadeloupe*, 1688. National Library of France, Paris.

Chocolate flavoured Anecdotes

During the 1914-1918 war, despite the considerable poverty of the general population, as always, housewives tried to compensate for the lack of luxury items and riches by providing substitutes. Thus, there was a Walloon family recipe for "wartime pralines", part of it reads as follows: Cook potatoes in their skin in unsalted water; pour through a very fine sieve to make mashed potatoes. Add sugar, butter, cocoa, breadcrumbs and almond essence. Mix well to obtain a homogeneous mass. Shape the mass into small pralines of any form desired, then roll in the cocoa. Cool before eating.

On 29 June 1995, cosmonauts and astronauts, the Russians and the Americans, met in space aboard the Mir orbiting station. They exchanged gifts, including chocolate!

Amélie Nothomb, a prize-winning Belgian author, commented recently in a 'Thank You' note after receiving a box of Neuhaus chocolates, "You should have seen my face when I received this huge box of chocolates: astonishment followed by the trembling anticipation of my fondness for chocolate."

→ Miss Margaret Parsons distributing hot chocolate and biscuits for children's tea-time, 1919. National Museum of Franco-American Cooperation, Blérancourt.

The transformation of chocolate

The cocoa pods turn brown

It would appear that the cocoa tree was planted by the Mayas in the northern part of Latin America some 600 years before the Christian era. This tree only grows in humid, hot and shady regions, preferably at an altitude of less than 600 metres. This defines the territory of the tropical zone of our planet between 22° latitude north and 21° latitude south. To the north is Cuba, and Reunion Island lies to the south.

The trees measure from 4 to 10 metres in height. Generally, they are not allowed to grow taller than 8 metres in order to facilitate picking the cocoa pods. The pods weigh between 200 and 800 grams and contain 10 to 50 cocoa beans. The cocoa pod looks like a thick shell with a length of some 30 cm; the colour changes as the fruit ripens. It goes from green or yellow to orange, red or brown. Of the 6,000 flowers on the cocoa tree, only 1% develops into a pod. The cocoa tree blooms from the age of three years, it blooms twice a year in June and October, and gives its full yield towards its seventh year; it becomes gradually less fruitful after 25 years. The ripening period for a cocoa pod, from fecundation to harvest, takes approximately 5-6 months. Harvesting the fruits of the cocoa tree consists of sectioning the pod's peduncle (generally using a machete, a pruning hook or pruning shears) and removing the beans. The cultivation of the cocoa trees is generally in the hands of small producers, cultivating less than 5 hectares or modest family operations. However, there are also vast domains and large plantations in countries such as Malaysia and Brazil. Cocoa trees are usually planted in lines with approximately 3 metres between them, which makes an average density of between 950 and 1,330 cocoa trees per hectare. However, this situation can vary significantly depending on the country, the fertility of the soil and the climate. To obtain maximum efficiency, the trees destined to protect the cocoa trees from the sun (as well as the installation of temporary shade, generally gliricidia or plantains) should be planted 6-9 months before the Theobroma cacao. The latter should be planted out during the first part of the rainy season to give the tranplants time to get stronger before the beginning of the dry season. Under normal circumstances, the average

← Harvesting cocoa pods in Madagascar.

yields for cocoa trees cultivated in the traditional manner vary between 300 and 500 kg per hectare. Some hybrid species can obtain yields of more than 1,000 kg per hectare. Climate conditions and risks of pathogens are the main exogenous factors that impact production.

It is estimated that approximately 30% of world production is affected by various diseases, insects, fungi and cocoa bean parasites. The most well known are black rot, witch's broom, and swollen shoot. When the harvest is in, the next stage is the fermentation: the beans are placed in trays covered with banana leaves. The temperature may vary between 45°C and 50°C. They are allowed to rest for about one week. Fermentation removes the pulp from the beans, reduces the bitter taste and develops the precursors of aroma. At this stage, they still contain 60% humidity which needs to be reduced to 7% to ensure the best preservation and transport conditions. The beans are then dried in the sun or in dryers and sometimes they are washed. They are then shipped.

Among the varieties of beans are the "criollo", an extremely good quality bean, which is yellowish brown; the "forastero", a brownish violet bean originating in the Amazon which is the most common bean given that it represents 80% of worldwide production; and the "trinitario", a hybrid of the two previous beans which was adopted after the destruction of the cocoa trees on Trinity Island by a cyclone in 1727.

↓ Cocoa beans being removed from the pods.

The cocoa mass

Transforming the cocoa beans into a mass requires three operations. Firstly, the roasting: the beans pass through hot air at a temperature between 120° and 140°C to separate them from the peel. This action is similar to the roasting of coffee beans or hazelnuts. A "roaster" surveys the degree of cooking; which is shorter or longer depending on whether a more pronounced or more subtle aroma is required. The crushing operation follows which consists of reducing the beans to particles of 2 to 3 mm. The peel is retrieved and is used by the food processing industry. The cocoa nib (*le grué*) is then passed through a series of cylinders that crushes it. The cellular tissue of the beans is torn and releases its 50% cocoa butter content, which is liquefied. The *grué* goes from being a solid to being a liquid, this is the cocoa mass. There are two options at this stage of the transformation, to produce cocoa powder or chocolate.

To obtain cocoa powder, the mass is alkalized, crushed, homogenised and the cocoa butter (to be used for the chocolate) is separated from the cocoa press cake (which will be crushed into powder).

Finally, conching is the last operation ('conching' comes from the Spanish word *concha* which means shell as this was the shape of the first cakes): the mass is poured into vats with a temperature varying from 50°C to 80°C, the cocoa butter is added to make it more fluid. This operation lasts from 2 to 4 days. A mixer inside the vat airs the liquid chocolate froth. The cocoa butter must coat every single particle of the mass in order that it is homogeneous and becomes creamy smooth and shiny. Thus the chocolate comes into being. The mass is kept in the liquid state at a temperature of 40°C.

Tempering is the next stage: the chocolate is cooled in accordance with a very precise temperature curve to obtain crystallisation. The technique of tempering the chocolate consists of melting it at 55°C then cooling it to 26°C and working it at a temperature of approximately 31-32°C for dark chocolate, 30-31°C for milk chocolate and 27-28°C for white chocolate. This achieves the perfect crystallisation of the chocolate without any marbling effect. If the tempering process is incorrectly carried out, the melting and cooling should be repeated as the chocolate does not lose any of its properties during the operation. The tempering can be carried out *"on marble";* the chocolate is then cooled directly on a marble slab. A spatula is used to homogenise the mixture and the operator merely has to put a drop of chocolate to his lips to verify the temperature or preferably use a thermometer. For reasons of hygiene, a tempering machine is frequently used to mix the chocolate respecting the crystallisation curves by varying the temperatures. The chocolate is thus always at the correct working temperature.

Dark chocolate is made of the cocoa mass, cocoa butter and sugar. Milk is added when making milk chocolate, and white chocolate is made of only cocoa butter, sugar and milk.

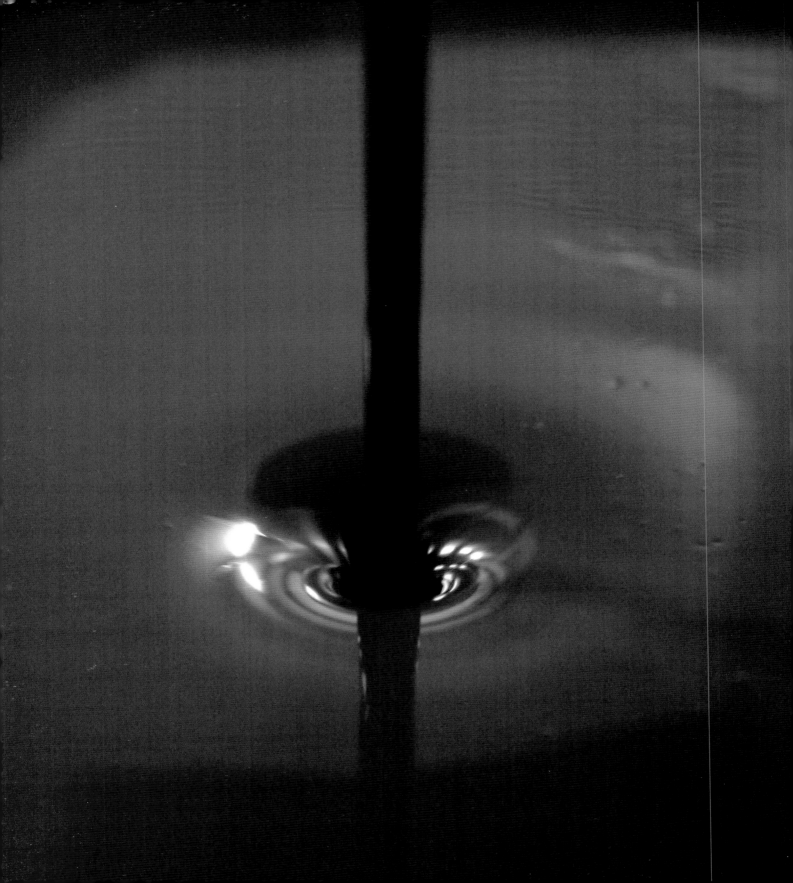

The alchemy of chocolate

Choices regarding quality can be made at all the stages, either concerning the ingredients, the amount of time taken for each stage, or based on the know-how of the chocolate maker. The very first quality choice is in the selection of the cocoa beans.

Let us introduce a brief digression to explain the care and attention given nowadays regarding the quality of the cocoa beans. The ICCO (International Cocoa Organisation) pays great attention concerning the various diseases that can attack the cocoa trees. For example, "witch's broom" which causes hypertrophy of the buds and provokes the characteristic aspect of a witch's broom. This is transmitted by the fungus *crinipellis perniciosa* that produces branches without fruit and non-viable leaves in the affected cocoa tree. The disease appeared in Ecuador in 1916, in Peru in 1930 and in Bahia in 1989. Successful action was taken in Brazil, Ecuador and Peru in 2004 and 2005 using molecular biology techniques to obtain varieties of cocoa tree resistant to this disease

The buyer of the beans also has to dose the mix. For a long while, the ideal mix was considered to be two-thirds Brazilian "marignan" and one-third Venezualan "caraque" and a pinch of "Cayenne pepper" to personalise the aroma.

All the doses that follow in the process are important too. The cocoa butter content makes the chocolate more or less dry. The proportion of sugar obviously makes it more or less sweet. The note of bitterness in dark chocolate must remain, it should never be neutral.

The genius of Van Houten

Without a doubt, the greatest discovery in the history of chocolate was made by the Dutchman Coenraad J. Van Houten. Today, chocolate would not exist in its present form without the genius of Van Houten. In 1828, he registered a patent for "chocolate powder". He had invented a press for extracting the cocoa butter and subsequently obtaining a dry powdery substance from which solid chocolate can be prepared. Until then, a major part of drinking chocolate was fats. That was the reason why it had to be beaten with a whisk to make the liquid froth, and then the fatty froth that rose to the surface had to be removed. In addition, in order to balance the high fat content, flour, corn, oats, etc. had to be added to the drink. Obviously, this particular liquid chocolate was far too nutritious.

Van Houten set up business in Amsterdam in 1815. A German scientist, J.M. Lehmann from Dresden, assisted him in his research. He was an eminent specialist in chocolate production material. He had also invented a process called "Dutching", copied from the Mayas' technique of adding ashes, which consisted of adding potash to the cocoa powder to make it more digestible.

Van Houten's invention made it possible to create chocolate tablets, bars, pralines, etc.... as by extracting the cocoa butter, it could then be added to a mixture of cocoa mass and sugar and then be moulded.

However, it was not until 1847 that Fry & Sons of Bristol, England, launched the world's first solid chocolate bar on the market!

Some other inventions

There are several particular developments in the creation of chocolate that need to be highlighted.

In 1875, Daniel Peter (1836-1919) invented milk chocolate. It was romance that led him to enter the chocolate business. The son of a butcher in Vevey, he fell in love with Fanny, the daughter of François-Louis Cailler, Switzerland's leading chocolate maker. Daniel Peter then decided to become a chocolate maker too. Thanks to the process of milk condensation, developed by another great Swiss, Henri Nestlé, he was able to introduce the world's first milk chocolate.

While several countries, including Switzerland and Belgium, were battling it out to be known as "THE country for chocolate", a brochure from Compagnie

↓ Chocolate production: "mixers", advertisement for the Moreuil company, *circa* 1900. Private collection.

Chocolat MOREUIL   Pl. 7

MÉLANGEURS

Internationale d'Alimentation, a chocolate producer in Bois d'Haine, Belgium, contained the following text: "We maintain that our chocolates are by no way inferior and can be compared with the best brands from other countries. It should be recognised that they have attained this level due to the little known fact that the milk from flat countries is superior in nutritional value to milk from mountainous lands." Enough said!

In 1879, another Swiss, Rudolph Lindt (1855-1909) who had a chocolate factory in Berne, invented the fundamental process of kneading and refining chocolate, which today is called "conching". In 1913, another Swiss, Jules Séchaud, launched the first chocolate with a filling. In 1921, the Belgian company Kwatta launched the chocolate bar.

In 1923, an American chocolate maker from Chicago, Mr. Frank Mars, created 'Milky Way', thereby launching a fashion for chocolate bars filled with choco-

↓ Chocolate manufacture: "sugar, sterilisation and pulverisation", advertisement for the Moreuil company, *circa* 1900. Private collection.

late that is still immensely popular today. In 1932, his son Forrest Mars developed the 'Mars' bar. This was swiftly followed by the launch of 'Nuts' in the Netherlands, a chocolate bar filled with hazelnuts and malt, and 'Kit-Kat' in the United Kingdom.

In 1933, an American discovered the chocolate chip biscuit by accident. Ruth Wakefield was running late and was quickly preparing some chocolate biscuits for her children, but she forgot to melt the chocolate first. She was not concerned about it, thinking that the chocolate would melt in the oven. However, it did not and the chocolate chip cookie was born! An American writer made this tasty observation, "Most chocolate chip cookies do not contain enough chocolate chips!"

Fry's Cocoa

Pure Concentrated

Chocolate Production

CACAO

The major cocoa countries

At the beginning of the 21st century, the three leading cocoa bean producing countries are Ivory Coast (1,273,000 tonnes of beans), Ghana (586,000 tonnes) and Indonesia (435,000 tonnes). They are followed by Nigeria, Brazil, Cameroun, Ecuador, Malaysia, Colombia, Mexico, Papua New Guinea, Dominican Republic, Peru, Venezuela and India. Worldwide, 3,289,000 tonnes of cocoa beans are produced per year. In 1830, world production of cocoa beans was a mere 10,000 tonnes. It was only in the 19th century, at the time of the rapid expansion of European manufacturing industries, that cocoa trees were introduced into Ecuador, Brazil, and Africa in 1822, driven by colonial ambition. South East Asia has only been cultivating cocoa trees since the 1970s, but it has made up for lost time! Today, the African continent provides almost 70% of worldwide cocoa bean production. In Central and South America, the production represents just 13% of world production. Finally, South East Asia, the most recent producer, is developing rapidly and is currently producing 17% of the world production.

The eight leading cocoa bean producing countries (Ivory Coast, Ghana, Indonesia, Nigeria, Brazil, Cameroun, Ecuador and Malaysia) produce 90% of the world's total production. Despite this strong concentration, the producer countries represent the weakest part of the sector and the most exposed to price variations; and the cocoa market is most definitely subject to price variations. For Ivory Coast, Ghana and Cameroun, cocoa sales are their principal source of export revenue. In Africa, some 11 million people, the producers and their families, grow cocoa trees on small family-owned plots of land. Growing the cocoa trees often constitutes their main source of income.

← Alfred Auguste Janniot, relief on the façade of the Colonies Museum built for the Colonial Exhibition, 1931. Quay Branly Museum, Paris.

The European Directive 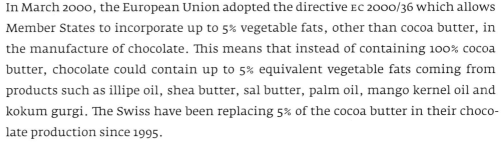 of the year 2000

→ Neuhaus can be proud
of being one of the first
companies to maintain
the original quality of
chocolate!

In March 2000, the European Union adopted the directive EC 2000/36 which allows Member States to incorporate up to 5% vegetable fats, other than cocoa butter, in the manufacture of chocolate. This means that instead of containing 100% cocoa butter, chocolate could contain up to 5% equivalent vegetable fats coming from products such as illipe oil, shea butter, sal butter, palm oil, mango kernel oil and kokum gurgi. The Swiss have been replacing 5% of the cocoa butter in their chocolate production since 1995.

The chocolate industry can thereby obtain less costly raw materials and the vegetable fats industry will acquire new markets. Nevertheless, this directive also allows those who wish to do so to continue producing real chocolate in accordance with the original recipes. The label "Ambao" is trying to indicate this on its packaging. The Neuhaus company can be proud of the fact that they are one of the first companies to have stated that they are maintaining their original quality!

Cocoa bean multinationals

The cocoa sector is highly concentrated. Five companies in the northern hemisphere control 80% of the world cocoa trade. The most powerful among these are Callebaut, ADM Cocoa and Cargill. Five western multinationals handle 70% of the transformation of cocoa; they are Callebaut, ADM Cocoa, Cargill, Nestlé and Hamester. Finally, six multinationals share 80% of the chocolate market. Of these six, three are American: Hershey, Mars and Philip Morris (which is the owner of Kraft-Jacobs-Suchard-Côte d'Or). The three others are European: the Swiss Nestlé, the British company Cadbury-Schweppes and the Italian Ferrero. Competition among these various giants is very keen. In order to increase their position in the market, the largest companies are gradually swallowing the smaller firms and their brands. For example, Côte d'Or was acquired by Jacobs Suchard, which in turn was acquired by Philip Morris.

↘ Harvesting cocoa pods in Madagascar.

The price of cocoa beans

The price of cocoa on the world market is fixed in the raw materials exchanges, mainly in London and New York. The mechanism used is that of supply and demand, i.e. market forces. When the cocoa supply is greater than the demand, the price declines and, conversely, when the supply is less than the demand, the price increases. Cocoa production is characterised by its lack of elasticity. In the short term, producers have very little room to manoeuvre in adapting their cocoa production to the demand. When the demand is high, producers can only respond by taking even greater care of their cocoa trees and by planting new trees which will need several years before they bear fruit for the first time. Thus, it would take a few years before the increased production can be realised. The consequent increase in the supply would then lead to a surplus in relation to the demand. The surplus cannot be sold in the short term and that puts pressure on prices. The decline in prices leads the producers to neglect their crops and cease the replacement of old trees. All this inevitably leads to a breakdown and then the same cycle starts again.

This is exactly what happened in the period 1970-1980. High prices in the second half of the 1970s led to an increase in production at the beginning of the 1980s. Prices then gradually declined to the point where the supply of cocoa could not meet the demand in 1991-1992.

Although cocoa is mostly produced by developing countries, it is essentially consumed in Europe, North America, Japan and Singapore (which also re-exports the derivative products after transformation). The principal outlets for the Latin American countries are the United States, whereas West Africa tends to export the greater part of its beans to Europe. Indonesia, Malaysia and certain Latin American countries, such as Ecuador, sell most of their harvest to Japan directly or via Singapore.

Consumption is estimated at 42.6% for Europe, 25.8% for America, 17.4% for Asia and Oceania and 14.2% for Africa.

In Belgium in 2003, every household spent approximately one-tenth of its household budget on food. In more detail, it emerged that 2% was spent on chocolate, 0.6% on pralines 0.3% on chocolate spreads. The Brussels region is the greatest chocolate consumer, and that is where the greatest number of specialist boutiques are located! The overall chocolate market in Belgium shows that candy bars are in the lead (30%), followed by pralines (22%), tablets (15%) and bars (12%).

→ Dried cocoa beans
ready for export.

Chocolate varieties

The different kinds of chocolate

Couverture chocolate is the name given to the chocolate that serves as the raw material for chocolate makers, confectioners and pastry cooks. It contains at least 31% cocoa butter and 12.5% dry cocoa with the fat removed. It is available either in the hot liquid form, delivered by tank trucks, or in the solid form. The solid form consists of flakes, pastilles, callets, etc. Mostly, it is presented in 5 kg blocks which are stored at a temperature of less than 18°C. The chocolate maker, Barry-Callebaut, for example, has more than 600 recipes for couverture chocolates which they keep for their clients.

There are four categories of chocolate tablets: pure chocolate, milk chocolate, white chocolate and chocolates with filling. The coating of the chocolates with filling must be at least one quarter of the total weight. In the milk chocolate category, there are nuances such as 'for everyday consumption' with 30% cocoa and 'superior' which has 43%, etc. The same criteria apply for chocolate bars.

Chocolate tablets and bars can have fillings. There are an infinite number of recipes, but there are a series of standard fillings. Fondant is a sugar syrup to which glucose has been added and it is then worked with a spatula until a white malleable consistency is achieved. Coffee, vanilla or fruit flavours can be used for flavouring. Ganache is a combination of cooked fresh cream and chocolate, to which a liqueur, or tea, or fruit can be added. Of course, there are other fillings such as nougat, marzipan, jellied fruit, crème de menthe, or liqueurs etc.

The diversity of pralines

A part of the manufacture of pralines is mechanised, however, there has always been part of the work done by hand, particularly the decoration. Two techniques are used in manufacturing pralines: moulding and coating. In the moulding process, liquid chocolate is poured into a hollow mould. The little cups obtained are cooled and then they harden. The desired filling, liquid or solid, is inserted and they are sealed with another layer of liquid chocolate. This will be the base of the praline. After cooling them again, they are removed from the mould. For the coating, as the name indicates, the filling is dipped into a bath of liquid chocolate or passed beneath a curtain of chocolate.

A multitude of variations are possible when making pralines, as the number is multiplied by the type of chocolate of the outer shell and by the type of filling inserted. Nevertheless, there are some classics in the history of the praline that have always pleased the clientele and gourmets. Thus, the range comprises eight fillings for the basic pralines in the three qualities: fondant, milk and white. Marzipan is a mixture of almonds and sugar. The best percentage of freshly peeled almonds is between 50-60%. The praliné is a mixture of roasted hazelnuts, almonds and/or other dried fruits, sugar and chocolate. Gianduja – an Italian invention from the Turin region – is a mixture of roasted hazelnuts, sugar and chocolate. Cocoa butter can also be added to it. The truffle is a mixture of butter, fondant sugar, chocolate and a liqueur. The fresh cream filling also contains chocolate and sometimes liqueur, tea or a fruit. Fondant sugar or confectionary is often used in the manufacture of other delicacies such cherries in kirsch or pralines with fresh cream. The liqueur filling is presented in two forms: the first, surrounded by a chocolate shell which releases three flavours, liqueur, chocolate and the fine film of crystallised sugar; and the second, with no chocolate shell and therefore no crystallised sugar. Then there is the particular case of "Manon", whose origin is uncertain. According to some, it is the case of a chocolate maker who never revealed his invention and

→ Manons coffee sugar.

← Previous pages:
Manufacturing process for
the *Caprice* and *Tentation*
pralines.

who may have created it in memory of *L'Histoire du chevalier des Grieux et Manon Lescaut*, the last volume of *Mémoires d'un homme de qualité* published in 1731 by Abbé Prévost. The lovelorn hero is torn between the passion of his love for a young woman and divine love. Manon, the heroine has become a myth of literature. Others think that the creator, just as anonymous, was inspired by the opera *Manon* by Jules Massenet, presented in 1884. The Neuhaus Manon is still filled with fresh cream or butter cream. It rests on a nougatine base (or marzipan, in white chocolate, etc.). Manon is decorated with a walnut kernel and is coated with vanilla or coffee flavoured fondant sugar. In the light of these details, experts call any praline made with fresh cream and coated in white chocolate a "false Manon"!

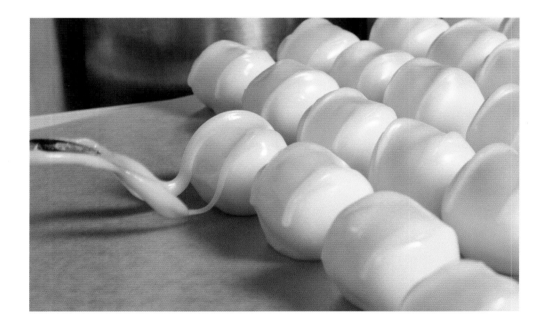

→ Manons vanilla sugar.

Strength is the capacity to break
a chocolate bar into four pieces with your bare hands –
and then eat just one of the pieces.

(Judith Viorst, American novelist)

Other forms of chocolate

Hollow chocolate figurines (made with moulds) are sold especially at Easter time and Christmas. Easter eggs have become a standard in the chocolate industry and among artisans. There are also small individually wrapped chocolate squares that are presented as an accompaniment to tea or coffee. These squares can be solid or mint truffles, such as the famous English "After Eights", or flavoured with spices, tea, etc.

Chocolate money is among the Belgian specialities (wrapped in silver or gold paper, or unwrapped), which vary depending on the commercial status of the currency, dollars or euros. It is amusing to recall that making chocolate money is really returning the product to its original purpose, since cocoa beans originally served as currency.

Chocolate cigarettes also had their hour of glory. There is now a European Union recommendation encouraging more and more countries to prohibit the production of chocolate cigarettes, as it could encourage children to smoke in the future. In his text *Save chocolate cigarettes*, the historian Gilles Dal pointed out the paradox in prohibiting chocolate cigarettes but not prohibiting cigarettes made of tobacco; he reminded us that chocolate cigarettes are chocolate and not cigarettes. He concluded with the following words: "We are living in a strange era when we talk of legalising soft drugs at the same time as we are prohibiting chocolate cigarettes!" We should add that in England, the industry is running trials of cigarettes that taste of chocolate, wine or vanilla. Some brands are already using certain perfumes, such as cocoa butter, in very small quantities that cannot be detected by the smoker.

Many artisans have taken up sculpting in chocolate and there is a broad range of these sculptures, including the classic Greek Discobole, a Brussels tram and the Eiffel tower! More recently, there have been incredible dresses made in chocolate or sprinkled with chocolate which have been among the highlights of chocolate fairs all over the world.

← Chocolate hat made by Daniel Stallaert.

Chocolate biscuits have been produced by industry since 1830, thanks to the English firm Huntley and Palmers. In Belgium, it was Edward De Beukelaere from the Polders who started a business in Antwerp in 1855, and who became the principal biscuit producer since 1870. Victoria and Parein were soon to follow and join the ranks of biscuit makers. Chocolate can be used in biscuit making as a filling or as a topping. In the first case, cocoa powder is added to the basic ingredients (sugar, fat). For the topping, take chocolate fondant or milk chocolate or more frequently a mixture of the two and coat a part of the biscuit or all the biscuit by dipping into a basin of hot chocolate.

There are chocolate flavoured beverages available in the form of an instant chocolate drink where the powder is mixed with milk, or in the ready-to-drink liquid form. In Belgium, 60,000,000 litres of chocolate flavoured drinks are purchased every year, divided as follows: 70% (mainly children under 12) drink instant chocolate and 30% (essentially the 15-24 age group) drink liquid chocolate. Product examples are Nesquik, Ovolmaltine and Kwatta for the powder format and Cécémel for the liquid product.

Finally, it is noteworthy that the Belgians are the biggest consumers of chocolate spreads with an average consumption of 800 g to 1 kg per year. 90% of these spreads have a hazelnut base and most of them are made by Ferrero (Nutella). Belgium exports as much to France as it imports from Italy and France.

A word of advice to chocolate fans

Chocolate releases the greatest amount of aroma when it is between 18°C and 21°C. Good chocolate should melt in the mouth; it should be fluid and creamy.

It should be kept at a constant temperature. A cellar would be a suitable place, just as for wine, but not a cellar that is damp, because humidity turns chocolate white. The ideal conservation temperature should be between 14°C and 18°C. When chocolate goes from hot to cold, it becomes white. When it goes from cold to hot, it sweats. Chocolate should be kept in a closed container or in silver foil; this prevents it from being impregnated with other odours.

Chocolate is a rich food and difficult to match with a drink. The great gastronomy experts of the 20th century, Escoffier and Curnonsky among others, all recommended water. When chocolate contains vanilla, coffee would be a good match. As for champagne, contrary to the received wisdom and legendary tales, it would seem that it does not go at all well with chocolate. With regard to wine, that depends on the type of chocolate. Dark chocolate (with 60% cocoa content) needs a relatively old sweet and natural wine, slightly maderized. Chocolate also goes well with a fruity cognac or full-bodied white wines. For milk chocolate, mellow whites and certain dry reds are recommended, but not the sweet natural wines. For bitter chocolate, according to some the king of chocolate, sweet natural red wines are a good match but no whites at all; as for spirits, a pure old malt whisky or a calvados.

The madness of chocolate

As in other sectors, chocolate has not escaped the craziness of outlandish records and peculiar deeds. Here are some of the strange things that have happened in recent years related to chocolate.

In the United States, where everything is outsize, the biggest chocolate fountain in the world is to be found in Oregon; it contains 2 tonnes of liquid chocolate. In New York, a couple were married in a bath filled with chocolate.

In Ringwood, Australia, an Easter egg was made that weighed 4.7 tonnes and was 7 metres high!

In Tokyo, Japan, a Swiss chocolate maker exhibited a chocolate bar that measured 221 metres in length! Here are two other Swiss records: in August 2001, a baker from Valais made the world's biggest chocolate éclair, it measured 503.74 metres in length; in Geneva in December 2002, people could drink the biggest bowl of hot chocolate in the world, the bowl contained 1,602 litres!

Every kind of chocolate pastry has its record and they are very impressive. In France alone: the biggest Chocolate Charlotte weighed 1,399 kg, it was made in Levallois; the biggest box of chocolates weighed 857 kg, it was 5 x 3.5 metres, it contained 17,748 chocolates and was built in Lyon in 1996; the biggest chocolate bell was made in Pornichet, it weighed 237.5 kg, was 1.87 metres high and had a diameter at the base of 2.12 metres; the longest chocolate Yule log was made in Epernay in 1989 and it measured 375 metres; a chocolate mousse weighing 90 kg was made in Grenoble; a Forêt Noire cake of 308 metres was prepared in Chambéry; at Plaisir, a school made the biggest chocolate truffle that weighed 780 kg! And the list goes on and on...

In the UK, Cadbury's, sponsors of the long-running TV series *Coronation Street* entrusted Aardman Animation, Oscar winning creators of Wallace and Gromit, to magically bring to life a "chocolate" image of Coronation Street, successfully achieving the look of a rich chocolate texture.

As a matter of curiosity, former American president Bill Clinton named his Labrador "Chocolate"!

The Art of Chocolate

A chocolate vocabulary

To find the origin of the words 'cacao' and 'chocolate', we have to go back to the Uto-Aztec Indian language of Central America which was the language of the Aztec Empire, which is still spoken today, *nahuatl* (or nahuat, or nahual). "Cacahuatl" means cocoa. The suffix "–atl" means water. The derivative of the word is "tlacacahuatl", with "tlalli", earth, meaning groundnut. The origin of the word is controversial. It probably comes from the verb "cacaua", to transmit among those who are working. As cocoa was cultivated by the Mayas before the arrival in their territory of peoples speaking the *nahuatl* language coming from the north, they probably transformed the word "cacau" into "cacahuatl". The Mayas had already designated the drink made from cocoa as "chacau haa", a beverage consumed during ceremonies. The Spanish therefore used the word "cacao" which then entered the French language in 1532 and "cacaoyer" in 1686. In 1722, a plantation was also called "cacaotière". The use of the term "cacao" to mean cocoa powder only dates back to 1903, and the adjective "cacaoté" to 1947. The Spanish word "chocolate", derived from *nahuatl*, entered the French language in 1598 and became "chocolat" in 1659. The word "chocolatière" appeared in 1671, "chocolatier" in 1694, the adjective "chocolaté" in 1771 and "chocolaterie" in 1867.

In 1870, the slang expression "c'est du chocolat!" meant "it's really great!" In 1896, a phrase that was repeated every night at the Nouveau Cirque by two successful clowns, Footit and Chocolat, "Je suis chocolat! ("I am great") became very widespread. Chocolat was the first "auguste" or fool in the history of the circus. His name was Raphael Padilla and he was born in Cuba in 1868 and died in Bordeaux in 1917. He has an incredible story: he was sold as a slave to a European and then became a servant to Tony Grice, a famous white-faced clown. Chocolat became extremely popular through his double act with Footit. Footit was born in 1864 in England and died in 1921. In their act, they made the most of the contrast between Chocolat's black skin (at that time, Chocolat was a derogatory term for black people) and Footit, the white-faced clown! Chocolat was the resident idiot, the fool. The expression "je suis chocolat", also became a slang term meaning "I am the accomplice". "Faire le chocolat" was synonymous with "faire le baron", i.e. to be an accomplice acting as a client so that the partner can fool the real clients. In this case, the "chocolat" is the sweetmeat that serves as bait.

In Belgium, you sometimes hear the expression "être chocolat bleu pale!" which has the same meaning.

In 1914, "être chocolat", i.e. to be black, meant to be inebriated.

Today, "tablettes de chocolat" is familiar language meaning an athlete's muscular and often tanned chest. Thus, in the poem "Midi 20", a new popular form of chanted poetry presented by "Grand Corps Malade", there is the line "Mes tablettes de chocolat sont devenues de la marmalade" (meaning "My rock hard chest has turned to jelly".)

→ Henri de Toulouse-Lautrec, *Chocolate dancing in a bar*, 1896. National Library of France, Paris.

CHOCOLAT DANSANT DANS UN BAR
Sois bonne ô ma chère inconnue !

Dessin de H. de TOULOUSE-LAUTREC.

19th Century literature

Honoré de Balzac (1799-1850) wrote about chocolate in his *Traité des excitants* in 1837, as did many other famous writers. It would, however, be amusing to find such comments in works of fiction.

Emile Zola (1840-1902) wrote in *Au bonheur des dames* (1837): "Since Paulette always had some sweetmeats in her pocket when she had to wait, she took out some chocolates and ate them with her bread."

In *Il ne faut jurer de rien*, Alfred de Musset (1810-1857) wrote, when the hero, Van Buck, seeing his poor but happy-go-lucky nephew, Valentin the dandy offer him a cup of chocolate, "What a breakfast! The devil take me! You live like a prince!" "Eh! What do you expect!" replied his nephew, "When you're starving to death, you have to find a way of enjoying yourself."

Gustave Flaubert (1821-1880) also introduced the theme of chocolate as an invigorating tonic; in *Madame Bovary* (1857) he wrote: "She must have her chocolate every morning, attentions without end. She constantly complained of her nerves, her chest and her liver. The noise of footsteps made her ill; when people left her, solitude became odious to her; if they came back, it was doubtless to see her die."

Guy de Maupassant (1850-1893) in one of his short stories *Ce cochon de Morin* (1882), published the following year in the collection *Contes de la Bécasse*, described this scene: "Someone knocked softly at my door. I asked: "Who's there?" A gentle voice replied: "Me." I got dressed quickly; I opened the door and she entered. "I forgot to ask you," she said, "what do you drink in the morning: chocolate, tea or coffee?" (...) At seven o'clock in the morning, she brought me a cup of chocolate. I had never tasted anything like it. A chocolate drink worth dying for, mellow, creamy, with an intoxicating aroma. I could not take my lips away from the delicious rim of the cup."

Chocolate was increasingly present everywhere, although in the 19th century, it still represented a luxury item to be served on special occasions. In *Petites filles modèles* (1857) by the Comtesse de Ségur, chocolate is featured, together with tea, and in *Poil-de-carotte* (1894) by Jules Renard, chocolate is associated with coffee.

← Sir John Lavery,
A cup of chocolate, 1888.
Private collection.

↓ Pierre Auguste Renoir,
The cup of chocolate, 1914.
The Barnes Foundation,
Merion, Pennsylvania.

Jean-Anthelme Brillat-Savarin

↑ Jean-Anthelme Brillat-Savarin, *The physiology of taste*, 1826.

→ Raimundo de Madrazo y Garetta, *Hot chocolate*. Private collection.

Jean-Anthelme Brillat-Savarin (1755-1826) is certainly the best known and the most brilliant critic and writer on gastronomy. It is therefore interesting to know his views on chocolate. He was the eldest of eight children, and was born in Belley in the department of Ain in France. He became interested in cooking through his mother who was an excellent cook. He had a double-barrelled name because one of his aunts made him her sole heir on the condition that he took her name.

Brillat-Savarin studied law in Dijon, in addition to some medicine and chemistry, and became a lawyer. He was elected deputy representing the Estates General at the National Constituent Assembly. He attracted attention following a speech against the abolition of the death penalty. He was a royalist and the revolutionary tribunal issued a summons against him, which forced him to go into exile in Switzerland and then the Netherlands, after which he spent two years in the United States

He discovered turkey in America and taught the art of making scrambled eggs to a French chef in Boston. He was allowed to return to France in 1796. He appreciated good restaurants, often invited people to dine at his home in Paris and also prepared several speciality dishes himself, such as tuna omelette, and filet steak with truffles. He caught a chill while attending a mass celebrated in memory of Louis XVI in the Saint-Denis basilica and died a few days later.

Two months before his death, a book appeared in bookstores that was to make him famous: *Physiologie du goût ou méditations de gastronomie transcendante, ouvrage théorique, historique et à l'ordre du jour, dédié aux gastronomes parisiens par un professeur, membre de plusieurs sociétés littéraires et savantes*, (The Physiology of Taste: or meditations on Transcendental Gastronomy; a theorical, historical and topical work, dedicated to the gastronomes of Paris by a professor, member of several literary and scholarly societies) (1825). Brillat-Savarin wanted to make the culinary art a veritable science. In the

book, he indulges in a very thorough analysis of the mechanism of taste. He is also a great raconteur of countless anecdotes, a defender of the delights of good food, all written in an elegant and amusing style.

The best pages of *The Physiology of Taste* relate Brillat-Savarin's observations on certain foods and their preparation, including coffee and chocolate. Among the author's quotations, the most well known is "Happy chocolate, which having circled the globe through women's smiles, finds its death at their lips." He also wrote: "If one swallows a cup of chocolate only three hours after a copious lunch, everything will be perfectly digested and there will soon be room for dinner." Elsewhere, we can read: "It is very suitable to persons who have much mental toil, to professors and lawyers, especially to travellers... Let every man who has passed in toil too much of the time when he should have slept; let every man of mind, who finds his faculties temporarily decay; every man who finds the air humid, the time long and the atmosphere painful to breathe; let them all take a half a litre of amber flavoured chocolate to 60 to 72 grains of amber per half kilogramme of chocolate, and they will see wonders!"

2oth century literature

Thomas Mann (1875-1955) wrote about chocolate in his first great work, a social novel set at the dawn of the 20th century *Buddenbrooks* (1901): "Breakfast in the small room overlooking the terrace! The morning air drifts in from the garden through the open glass door and, instead of being served coffee or tea, a cup of chocolate is served, yes, really, every day; the birthday drink of chocolate is served together with a thick slice of creamy brioche."

Yet gradually, the image of chocolate would become more banal, it would have to assimilate all its functions, that of the drink of the gods, of the nobility, of the upper middle classes, and of being medication – it was to go through a less glorious period at the beginning of the 20th century – to return once more to the role it had never ceased to play: being a sublime food and drink, which brings together with the pleasures of eating and drinking, a thousand advantages, especially the gift of bringing back childhood memories.

↓ Henri Matisse, *Still life with chocolate pot*, 1900. Private collection.

Raymond Queneau (1903-1976) remembered in *Chêne et chien* (1937): "You smeared chocolate all over your Sunday best clothes, with the excuse that aunty had forgotten your toy soldiers."

Marcel Proust (1871-1922) wrote in *Swann's Way* (1913): "When it was all finished, composed especially for us, but dedicated more particularly to my father who was an amateur, we were offered a chocolate cream, an inspiration, Françoise was being very attentive. It was ephemeral and light, and very suitable, and she had invested all her talent. To refuse to taste it or to leave one single drop in the dish would have been extremely impolite, just as boorish as getting up and leaving before the end of a piece, right under the nose of the composer."

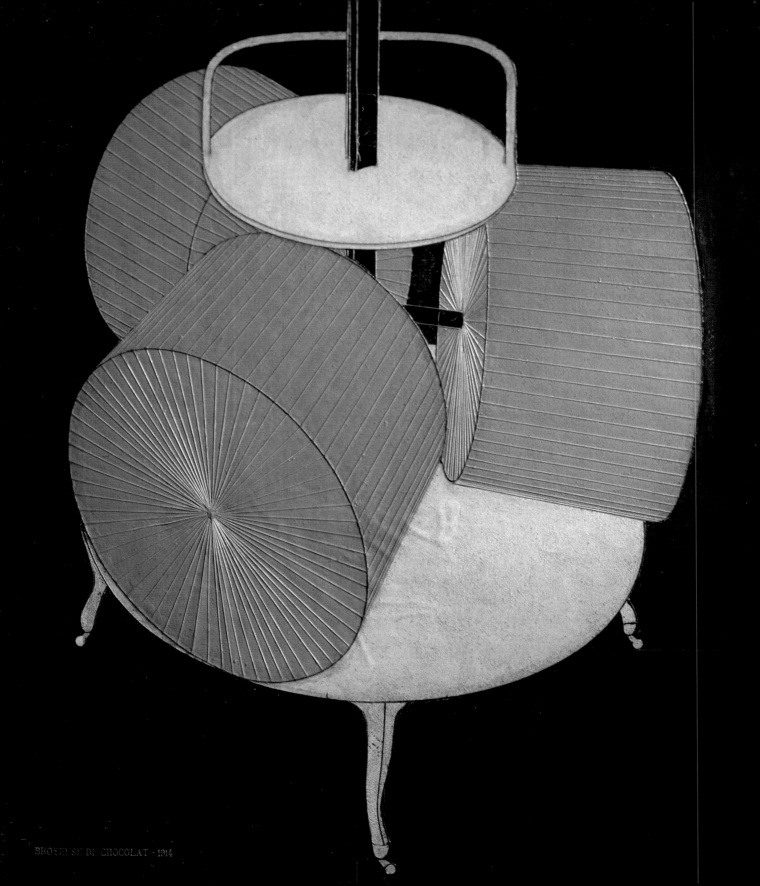

BROYEUSE DE CHOCOLAT - 1914

Colette (1873-1954), retracing the various stages of her own life, through book after book, described in *La maison de Claudine* (My mother's House) (1922): "It was night, about three o'clock in the morning, when the daily insomnia lit the lamp, opened the book on my mother's bedside table once more; the huge spider woke too, taking measurements like a surveyor, leaving the ceiling on a thread, immediately above the oil-lamp where, all night long, a bowl of chocolate had been growing cold. The spider descended, slowly, balancing gently like a large pearl; it gripped the edge of the bowl firmly with its eight legs and leaning forward it dipped its head into the chocolate and drank until it was satiated. Then, it climbed up again, its body heavy with the creamy chocolate, stopping frequently for the meditation imposed by a heavy stomach, and finally it returned to its place at the centre of its silken rigging."

At the same period, James Joyce (1882-1941) wrote in his monumental tome *Ulysses* (1922): "He poured into the two teacups two level spoonfuls, four in all, of Epps cocoa powder, and following the instructions on the packet, after the time required for the infusion, he proceeded to add to each cup, the ingredients specified in the manner and proportions indicated."

Jean-Claude Bologne is the author of a brilliant book *Histoire morale et culturelle de nos boissons* (1991), in which he explains, beyond the sometimes surreal disputes (if you drink chocolate, have you broken your fast?), that drinks are profoundly anchored in our customs and cultures. In his novel *La faute des femmes* (1989), he describes the sheer pleasure of preparing a bowl of chocolate: "The contrast between the warmth of the milk and the cold mass, between the liquid and the solid, the bitter and the sweet, took me to the edge of pleasure. The attraction of the forbidden lurked here."

← Marcel Duchamp, *The chocolate grinder no 2*, 1914. Philadelphia Museum of Art, Pennsylvania.

↓ Josef Hoffmann, silver-plated chocolate pot, *circa* 1906. Private collection.

Mama always said
life was like a box of chocolates,
you never know what you're gonna get.

(Forrest Gump,1994)

From the book to the cinema

Lasse Hallström, *Chocolat*, 2001. Royal Film Library, Brussels.

It is intriguing that in the Alfred Hitchcock film starring Anthony Perkins and Janet Leigh, *Psycho* (1960), deliberately filmed in black and white, in the critical scene where the heroine is spied on through a hole in the wall while taking a shower and is then brutally stabbed to death with a knife, the blood that trickles into the bath was in reality chocolate syrup! The film was adapted from the novel by Robert Bloch entitled *Psycho*.

Another legendary adaptation was *Charlie and the Chocolate Factory* (2005), based on the children's book by Roald Dahl, written in 1967 (13 million copies sold!). Tim Burton was the director of the film which starred Johnny Depp. As for the author Roald Dahl, he said, "If I were the headmaster of a school, I would get rid of the history teacher and replace him or her with a chocolate teacher; my pupils would study at least one subject that concerns us all".

In 1932, a Marc Allégret film, called *La petite chocolaterie* starring Raimu was released in France. The story features the daughter of a chocolate maker. In 1941, a musical film featuring a star of the Opéra was released with the title *The chocolate Soldier*.

Robert Zemeckis, *Forrest Gump*, 1994. Royal Film Library, Brussels

In the United States, Robert Zemeckis, the director of *Romancing the Stone*, *Back to the Future* and *Who framed Roger Rabbit?* has the hero say in his famous film *Forrest Gump* (1994): "Mama always said life was like a box of chocolates, you never know what you're gonna get."

In *Chocolat* (2000), a Lasse Hallström film starring Juliette Binoche and Johnny Depp (who admitted eating too many truffles during the shooting), the story tells of the opening of a chocolate boutique which will turn a small provincial town upside down. The reason is that chocolate led to sinning, gluttony, and idleness entering the community!

Among the other films in which the word 'chocolate' is mentioned, there is the Italian film *Bread and Chocolate* (Pane e Cioccolata) (1974) by Franco Brusati with Nino Manfredi and Anna Karina and the film "Chocolat chaud" (1998), adapted from the novel by Rachid O, in which hot chocolate symbolises for a young Moroccan the supreme happiness and sweetness of living in France.

Chocolat (1988), the film by Claire Denis with Isaach de Bankolé features the colonial period in Cameroun and a black boy.

↙ Tim Burton, *Charlie and the Chocolate Factory*, 2005. Warner Bros, Burbank, California.

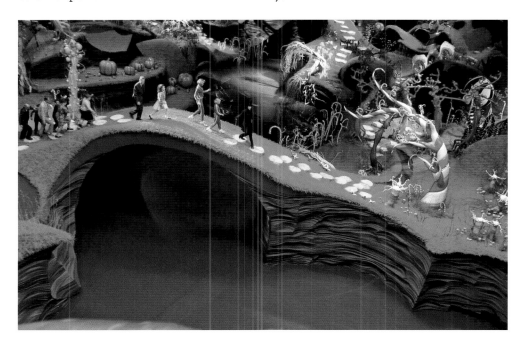

"Les mangeuses de chocolat"

↑ Philippe Blasband, *The chocolate eaters*, 1996.

They find chocolate irresistible, it makes them salivate, melt and tremble, but is it somehow ruining their lives? Chocolate, while evolving from fondness to pleasure, has become a drug. In order to be free of this addiction, four women participate in a group therapy session. Are they aware of what is behind their obsession with chocolate? This is the theme of the play "Les mangeuses de chocolat" (The chocolate eaters) by Philippe Blasband. A tragedy with no way out but tempered by humour, it was presented at the Avignon Festival in 2002 and was very successful.

In the famous play by the Scottish writer James Barrie (1860-1937), *Peter Pan*, the anecdote about the little boy who loved chocolate is true. Sylvia Llewelyn-Davies said to her son one evening, "If you carry on eating so much chocolate, you will be ill tomorrow...", and the child replied "I will be ill tonight!" The child in question, who did in fact exist, received one halfpenny in royalties for every performance of the play (created in 1904 and adapted by the author as a novel in 1911; and subsequently turned into a Disney film in which all the cruel aspects were eliminated)!

Worthy of mention too is the comic opera *Au bonheur du chocolat* (The joys of chocolate) by Katherine Khodorowsky, interpreted by the company La Marmite à Malices, an ode to the divine beverage, created in Paris in 2005.

The lyrics of Mathias Malzieu's song "Trim my hips with an axe – I have eaten too much chocolate... Knead my hips with kisses, I am becoming the chocolate woman" made the song *La femme chocolat* (The chocolate woman) a lively hit for Olivia Ruiz. In 2005, the beautiful Hadise, who was eating chocolate every day during the studio recording sessions, inspired this comment from the producer: "What is this thing that all of you have with chocolate!" This sparked off an idea for the hit number that was written the next day, *Milk Chocolate Girl*. Then in 1985, there was *Cho ka ka o* by Annie Cordy and *Les bêtises* by Sabine Paturel which starts with "J'ai tout mangé le chocolat" (I've eaten all the chocolate). We can also go back to the lullabies of our early childhood with "Fais dodo Colas mon petit frère, papa est en bas qui fait du chocolat" (Sleep, Colas, my little brother, Papa is downstairs and he's making chocolate….".

To confirm this obsession, here are some comments made by several celebrities about chocolate:

"Nine people out of ten love chocolate, the tenth person is lying!" (John G. Tullius, American artist and comic strip illustrator, born 1953).

"Strength is the capacity to break a chocolate bar into four pieces with your bare hands – and then eat just one of the pieces." (Judith Viorst, American novelist, born 1931)

"Do not believe that chocolate is a substitute for love. Love is a substitute for chocolate." (Miranda Ingram)

↓ Philippe Blasband, *The chocolate eaters*, poster by Pierre Holemans, 2004.

193

The flavours of Neuhaus chocolate

LE BAPTÊME

AU THÉATRE

LES DINERS

EN VOYAGE

The grand praline families

Prestigious pralines are still prepared using authentic recipes and respecting the artisan tradition of the Neuhaus house.

There are ten grand families of pralines, which are described as follows:

The first family is "Manon-Caprice-Tentation". We would like to highlight the two mythical pralines, one of which has given its name to the title of this book.

Tentation was created in 1958. It is made of nougatine with a filling of coffee flavoured ganache (mixture of cream and chocolate). It is coated with milk chocolate.

Caprice is made of nougatine, filled with vanilla fresh cream and coated with dark chocolate.

← Caprice praline section view.

← Previous pages : 1930 : the Neuhaus Collection.

Tentation
Nougatine with a filling of coffee flavoured ganache

Caprice
Nougatine filled with vanilla fresh cream

Manon sucre vanille (or café) was created in 1937. Beneath its cape of vanilla sugar (or coffee), hides a vanilla (or coffee) butter cream on a nougatine base and topped with a pecan nut. The Republic of Guinea is a country in north-west Africa. For a long time, the cocoa from there was considered the best that there is on the African continent. One ethnic group makes up a part of the population: the Manon. Perhaps this is the origin of the word 'Manon'?

Manon noir was created in 1990 and is made of a chocolate mousse resting on a chocolate pastille and coated with chocolate fondant. The secret that makes this product unique is the chocolate mousse centre – this is a return to childhood!

Manon Lait, also created in 1990, is made of butter cream, praliné and fragments of caramelised hazelnuts, resting on a chocolate pastille and coated with milk chocolate. If the origin of the word is not African, perhaps it comes from Manon Lescaut, the heroine of *L'histoire du Chevalier des Grieux et de Manon Lescaut*, the last volume of *Mémoires et aventures d'un homme de qualité* (1731) by Abbé Prévost. This work perhaps inspired *Manon*, the opera composed by Jules Massenet and performed in 1884.

There remain **Manon Choco café**, with its coffee butter cream and **Manon Choco vanille**, with a vanilla butter cream topped with a nut.

Manon

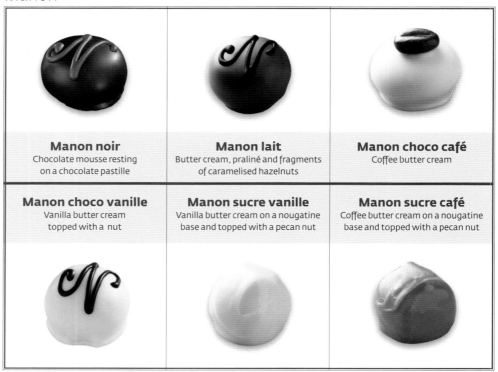

Manon noir	Manon lait	Manon choco café
Chocolate mousse resting on a chocolate pastille	Butter cream, praliné and fragments of caramelised hazelnuts	Coffee butter cream
Manon choco vanille	**Manon sucre vanille**	**Manon sucre café**
Vanilla butter cream topped with a nut	Vanilla butter cream on a nougatine base and topped with a pecan nut	Coffee butter cream on a nougatine base and topped with a pecan nut

The second family is the gianduja family, (gianduja is an Italian creation).

Gianduja Astrid was invented in 1937. A mixture of hazelnuts, sugar, milk and cocoa butter; this gianduja also contains butter and "candied sugar" in a sugar syrup to maintain the richness. Arriving in Belgium in 1926, Princess Astrid of Sweden won the hearts of the Belgian people. She died tragically in an accident in Switzerland in 1935. This praline was created to pay homage to her memory.

Gianduja Pagode dates back to 1958. It is a small chocolate cup made of chocolate fondant with a filling of coffee ganache (a mixture of cream and chocolate). The decoration is a gianduja. 1958 was the year of the Universal Exhibition in Brussels. Considerable interest was shown in Thailand's pavilion, which represented the pagoda style prevalent in that country.

That leaves the **Troïka**, made of marzipan and gianduja coated with sugar glaze, the **Millénaire**, gianduja with crisped rice, the **Gianduja café**, the **Bloc gianduja**, a pure gianduja, the **Cornet doré**, a gianduja decorated with almonds and hazelnuts, and the **Millionnaire**, a gianduja with crisped rice, noticeable for its chocolate lines and its white chocolate coating.

Gianduja

Troïka	Pagode	Millénaire	Astrid
Marzipan and gianduja coated with sugar glaze	Coffee ganache and gianduja	Gianduja with crisped rice	Gianduja with butter and "candied sugar"

Gianduja café	Bloc gianduja	Cornet doré	Millionnaire
Gianduja with coffee	Pure gianduja	Gianduja decorated with almonds and hazel nuts	Gianduja with crisped rice

The third family is the "fresh cream" family.

The **Fabiola** praline was created in 1960; it is a dark chocolate with vanilla fresh cream and dark ganache. Naturally, this praline was created in honour of Doña Fabiola de Mora y Aragon, who married the Belgian King Baudouin on 15 December 1960.

The **Baudouin** praline, created in the same year, is a moulded praline with a milk chocolate filling made of vanilla fresh cream. Baudouin I was the fifth king of the Belgians. During his reign, the King Baudouin Foundation was created with the objective of improving the living conditions of the Belgian people. King Baudouin died in 1993.

That leaves **Desdémone**, "fresh cream" with vanilla butter on a base of gianduja covered with a trace of dark chocolate; **Othello**, "fresh cream" with coffee butter on a gianduja base; **Aphrodite**, "fresh cream" with vanilla butter on a gianduja base, **Diane**, chocolate mousse on a gianduja base, and **Black & White**, "fresh cream" with fresh butter and hazelnuts.

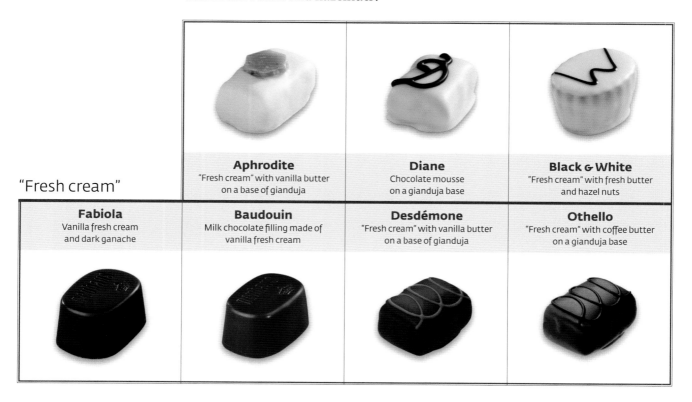

"Fresh cream"

Aphrodite "Fresh cream" with vanilla butter on a base of gianduja	**Diane** Chocolate mousse on a gianduja base	**Black & White** "Fresh cream" with fresh butter and hazel nuts

Fabiola Vanilla fresh cream and dark ganache	**Baudouin** Milk chocolate filling made of vanilla fresh cream	**Desdémone** "Fresh cream" with vanilla butter on a base of gianduja	**Othello** "Fresh cream" with coffee butter on a gianduja base

Pralinés

Paola Praliné and a whole roasted hazel nut	**Albert** Praliné and a whole roasted hazel nut	**Satan** Praliné filling and a hazel nut and almond base	**Méphisto** Praliné filling and a hazel nut and almond base
Noix double Praliné and caramelised hazelnuts	**Fruits de mer** Hazel nut praliné in the form of a shell	**Dollar** Soft hazel nut praliné	**Dollar** Soft hazel nut praliné

The fourth family is the most important one and includes the pralinés.

The **Paola** praline was created in 1959. It is a milk chocolate shell with a filling of a praliné (hazelnut and sugar), a mixture of chocolate and cocoa butter, as well as a whole roasted hazelnut. 1959 was the 'white wedding year' for the Belgian royal dynasty, just two years after Prince Albert first met Donna Paola Ruffo di Calabria, who came from an Italian noble family. It was the year of Salvatore Adamo's song "Dolce Paola", which reflected so well the feelings of the entire Belgian population.

The **Albert** praline is the same with a dark chocolate shell. Prince Albert and Donna Paola married on 2 July 1959. He is now the sixth king of the Belgians.

Satan dates from 1960. It is a praliné made of dark chocolate with a praliné filling and a hazelnut and almond base, with some fragments of caramelised hazel-

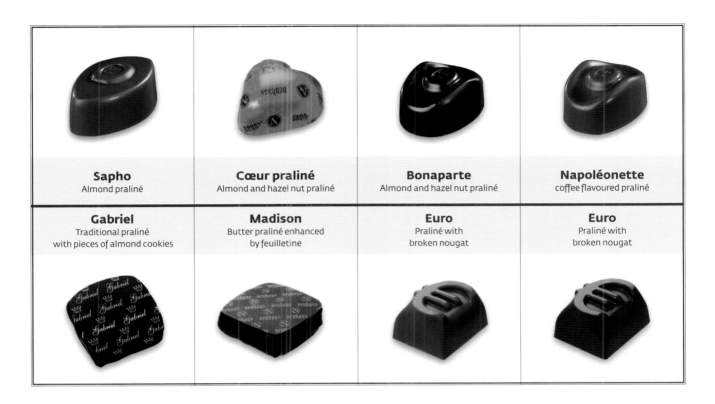

Sapho	Cœur praliné	Bonaparte	Napoléonette
Almond praliné	Almond and hazel nut praliné	Almond and hazel nut praliné	coffee flavoured praliné
Gabriel	**Madison**	**Euro**	**Euro**
Traditional praliné with pieces of almond cookies	Butter praliné enhanced by feuilletine	Praliné with broken nougat	Praliné with broken nougat

nuts. **Méphisto** (the same praline but made with milk chocolate) was created at the same time. Satan owes its name to its gloomy and dark side. Mephistopheles signed a pact with Faust in Goethe's famous play.

That leaves **Noix double**, praliné and caramelised hazelnuts; **Fruits de mer**, a hazelnut praliné in the form of a shell; **Dollar**, a soft hazelnut praliné bearing the dollar sign, in milk or dark chocolate; **Sapho**, an almond praliné in the shape of a lozenge; **Cœur praliné**, an almond and hazelnut praliné wrapped in red paper; **Bonaparte**, an almond and hazelnut praliné in the shape of a three-cornered hat; **Napoléonette**, a praliné of the same shape but coffee flavoured; **Gabriel**, a traditional praliné with pieces of almond cookies.

Madison, a butter praliné enhanced by feuilletine, and **Euro**, a praline with broken nougat bearing the euro sign and available in milk and dark chocolate.

Snobinettes

Snobinette champagne	**Snobinette capuccino**	**Snobinette noisette**
Champagne marc butter cream with grilled hazel nuts	Coffee butter cream	Praliné of almonds and grilled hazel nuts

The fifth family is the Snobinette family. There are three of them: **Snobinette champagne**, made from champagne marc butter cream with grilled hazelnuts; **Snobinette capuccino**, coffee butter cream; and **Snobinette noisette**, a praliné of almonds and grilled hazelnuts.

The sixth family is the caramel-ganaches family and it includes one of the oldest pralines of the Neuhaus house.

    Bonbon 13 was created in 1937, although it was only patented in 1948. It is a little chocolate fondant cup with a filling of ganache (mixture of cream and chocolate), gianduja and rum. The milk chocolate coating is completed by the figure 13 written in dark chocolate.

    That leaves **Violetta**, a ganache flavoured with violets and decorated with a crystallized violet petal from Toulouse, **Apothéose**, a ganache with roasted hazelnuts, **Prestige**, with caramel and **Criollo**, a bitter chocolate made with fresh butter.

Caramel – Ganaches

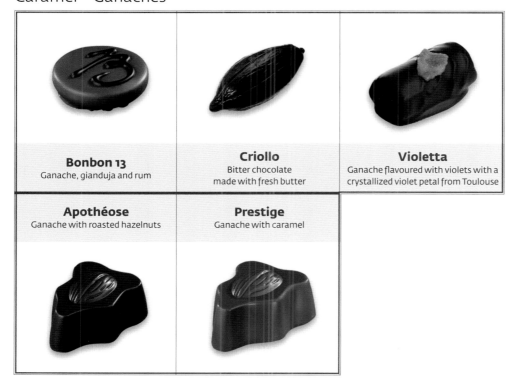

Bonbon 13 Ganache, gianduja and rum	**Criollo** Bitter chocolate made with fresh butter	**Violetta** Ganache flavoured with violets with a crystallized violet petal from Toulouse
Apothéose Ganache with roasted hazelnuts	**Prestige** Ganache with caramel	

The seventh family is the passion praline family. Here we find **Passion amande sucrée salée**, gianduja and caramelised salted almonds, **Passion ganache amère**, a pure bitter ganache, **Passion Mandarine**, a ganache flavoured with Mandarine Napoléon liquor, **Passion massepain nougat**, marzipan, nougatine and cognac, **Passion gingembre orange**, ganache made with ginger and orange, **Passion poire cannelle**, a ganache made with pear and cinnamon, and **Passion gianduja feuilletine**, a gianduja with feuilletine.

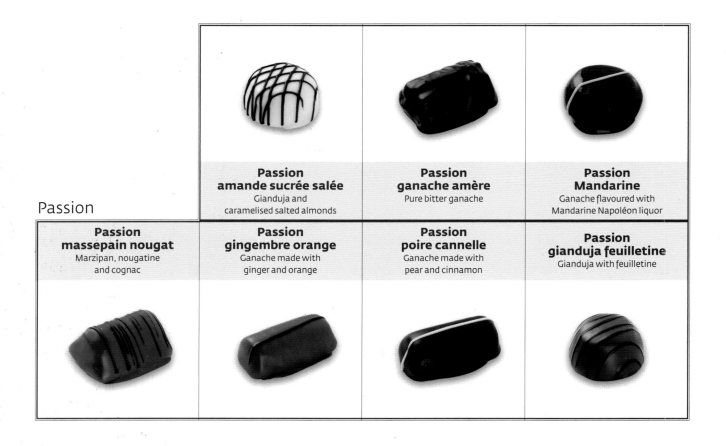

Passion

	Passion amande sucrée salée Gianduja and caramelised salted almonds	**Passion ganache amère** Pure bitter ganache	**Passion Mandarine** Ganache flavoured with Mandarine Napoléon liquor
Passion massepain nougat Marzipan, nougatine and cognac	**Passion gingembre orange** Ganache made with ginger and orange	**Passion poire cannelle** Ganache made with pear and cinnamon	**Passion gianduja feuilletine** Gianduja with feuilletine

Truffles

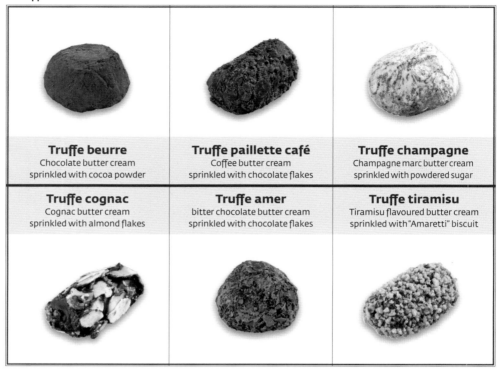

Truffe beurre	Truffe paillette café	Truffe champagne
Chocolate butter cream sprinkled with cocoa powder	Coffee butter cream sprinkled with chocolate flakes	Champagne marc butter cream sprinkled with powdered sugar
Truffe cognac	Truffe amer	Truffe tiramisu
Cognac butter cream sprinkled with almond flakes	bitter chocolate butter cream sprinkled with chocolate flakes	Tiramisu flavoured butter cream sprinkled with "Amaretti" biscuit

The truffles family is the eighth family and comprises the **Truffe beurre**, chocolate butter cream sprinkled with cocoa powder, **Truffe paillette café**, coffee butter cream sprinkled with chocolate flakes, **Champagne truffle**, champagne marc butter cream sprinkled with powdered sugar, **Cognac truffle**, Cognac butter cream sprinkled with almond flakes, **Truffe amère**, bitter chocolate butter cream sprinkled with chocolate flakes, and **Tiramisu truffle**, Tiramisu flavoured butter cream sprinkled with "Amaretti" biscuit.

The marzipan family is one of the last; it consists of **Canasta**, marzipan; **Carré Pistache**, pistachio marzipan with crystallised sugar enhanced with a pistachio nut; **Carré café**, decorated with a chocolate coffee bean; **Carré amande**, decorated with an almond, **Carré baie rose**, enhanced with a pink peppercorn, and **Carré noisette**, enhanced with a hazelnut.

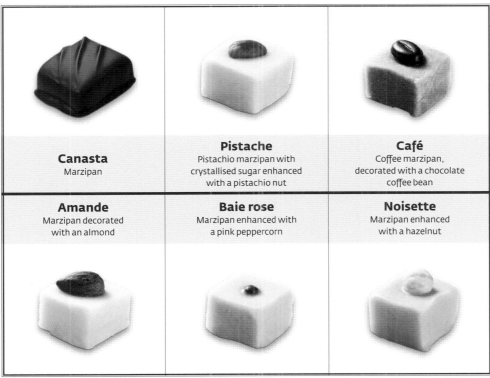

Canasta Marzipan	Pistache Pistachio marzipan with crystallised sugar enhanced with a pistachio nut	Café Coffee marzipan, decorated with a chocolate coffee bean
Amande Marzipan decorated with an almond	Baie rose Marzipan enhanced with a pink peppercorn	Noisette Marzipan enhanced with a hazelnut

Marzipan

The **Liqueurs** assortment are the pralines wrapped in paper of the same colour as the liqueurs Grand Marnier, Pear, Rum Cointreau, Cognac, etc.

The fruit family includes **Fraise des bois**, wrapped in red paper, a sugar cream fondant with strawberry pulp, **Paillette**, crystallized orange peel coated with chocolate, **Mendiant**, a great favourite with dried fruits, and **Cerisette**, a cherry with the stalk and stone macerated in alcohol.

Liqueurs

Liqueurs
Poire William, Rhum Saint-James, Grand Marnier, Whisky J&B,
Mandarine Napoléon, Cointreau, Cognac Bisquit, Vodka Smirnoff

Fruit

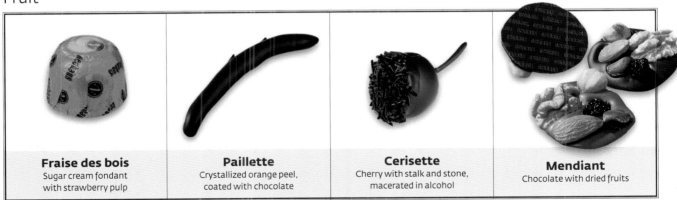

Fraise des bois	**Paillette**	**Cerisette**	**Mendiant**
Sugar cream fondant with strawberry pulp	Crystallized orange peel, coated with chocolate	Cherry with stalk and stone, macerated in alcohol	Chocolate with dried fruits

Other forms of chocolate

Neuhaus also offers a broad range of tablets that contain the standard flavours, and also **Coffee** (white chocolate), an interesting alchemy between the sweet flavour of white chocolate and the powerful flavour of the freshly roasted coffee bean; **Nuts & Nougats** (milk chocolate), a refined mix of milk chocolate, the best nougat and hazelnut chips; **Orange chocolate** (extra dark), a combination of a good 'vintage' selected chocolate and the bittersweet taste of the orange.

There is also an "origin" range where the cocoa beans are selected according to their precise origin to give the chocolate a unique flavour and a strong personality: **Madagascar**, a powerful chocolate made milder by the Bourbon vanilla creamy milk; **Occumare Vénézuela**, a mild chocolate flavoured with red peppercorns; **West Africa**, a harmony of powerful flavours that evoke coffee and coffee roasting; **Sao Tomé**, from the name of the island situated off the West African coast with flavours such as bitter, boisé and a mineral note.

There is also a range of chocolates with "no added sugar" and a whole selection of plain or filled chocolate bars.

Some chocolate recipes

At Neuhaus, the primarily artisan creations are made using top quality ingredients while showing every respect for tradition. "Cuisine de Jean Neuhaus" can give you several secrets concerning the preparation of chocolate sweetmeats. The kitchen range comprises fruit spreads, spreads for sandwiches, honey, flakes, cocoa powder, "snobbies", rocks and chocolat twigs.

Shortbread tartlets with fruit spread, finish with flakes

Ingredients for 30 tartlets

250 g butter, 5 g icing sugar, 275 g flour, 50 g dark cocoa, 1 egg, 1 egg yolk, Pinch of salt
200 g of fruit spread (forest fruits or raspberries), ½ litre sweetened fresh cream, Flakes
Small tart baking tins

Preparation (1 hour and allow 1 night for the dough to rest)

1 Mix all the ingredients to obtain a consistent dough mixture.
2 Allow dough to cool in the fridge during one night.
3 Flatten the cooled dough to a thickness of 3 mm.
4 Grease the tins and place dough mixture in them, pressing firmly in the corners of tins.
5 Fill with the fruit spread and bake for 10 minutes at 180°C.
6 After baking, allow to cool.

Finish

Beat the sweetened fresh cream and decorate tartlets with it.
Sprinkle the flakes all over the tartlets.

Chocolate biscuit coated with ganache

Ingredients, serves 8

FOR THE CHOCOLATE BISCUIT: *4 eggs, 4 egg yolks, 300 g sugar, 225 g flour, 50 g cocoa fondant, Raspberry fruit spread, Baking tin with loose bottom*

FOR THE GANACHE: *150 g fresh cream, 9 pieces of Rock (chocolat fondant) = 125 g, 50 g butter*

Preparation (90')

GANACHE:

1 Pour the fresh cream into a saucepan with a handle and bring to the boil.
2 Place the rocks in an ovenproof dish and pour the very hot fresh cream onto the rocks.
3 Add the butter last, taking great care.

Preparation of the biscuit

1 Beat the eggs, egg yolks and sugar to obtain a light frothy mixture.
2 Sift the flour and cocoa powder through a sieve,
    then add to the mixture by mixing with a spatula.
3 Grease baking tin, sprinkle with flour then pour the mixture into the tin.
4 Bake the biscuit for 30 minutes in a pre-heated oven at 220°C.
5 Allow the biscuit to cool and then cut lengthwise and
    cover with the raspberry fruit spread.
6 Close it and allow to cool for 10 minutes in the refrigerator.

Finish

Heat the ganache and coat the biscuit with the warm ganache.
Place some chocolate twigs in the centre of the biscuit for decoration.

Peppery hot milk chocolate

Ingredients for 1 litre

7.5 dl milk, 1 vanilla pod, 1 box of Rocks = 220 g dark chocolate,
½ red chilli pepper with seeds removed, 25g acacia honey, 1 pinch of Guérande salt

Preparation (15')

1 Boil milk and vanilla pod cut in two lengthwise in a saucepan with a handle.
2 Remove saucepan from the heat and set aside for 10 minutes.
3 Remove the vanilla pod and melt the chocolate in the milk.
4 Add the honey, salt and the finely chopped half red pepper.
5 Allow the mixture to rest for a few minutes.
6 Filter through a sieve and serve.

Recommendation

Pour the chocolate into pre-heated tumblers, add fresh cream
and sprinkle with flakes or cocoa fondant.

A selection of different recipes for Hot Chocolate

Mint flavoured hot chocolate

1 litre of full milk, 1 dessert spoon of honey, 4 sprigs of fresh mint,
10 teaspoons of Neuhaus cocoa powder, 5-8 cl of mint liqueur

1 Bring the milk, honey and mint leaves to the boil.
2 Filter using a sieve, add the cocoa powder and the mint liqueur and
   mix vigorously so that the mixture becomes frothy.
3 Serve in a cup, and decorate with a mint leaf.

Orange flavoured hot chocolate

1 litre of full milk, 1 orange with untreated peel, 10 teaspoons of Neuhaus cocoa powder,
5-8 cl of orange liqueur (Cointreau, triple sec or Mandarine Napoléon)

1 Wash the orange under hot water and cut into small pieces.
2 Bring the milk to the boil with the pieces of orange.
3 Filter using a sieve and add the liqueur.
4 Mix vigorously before serving.

This hot chocolate is delicious served with *orangette*
(a strip of orange peel coated with chocolate).

Gourmet

75 cl of full milk, 25 cl single cream, half a vanilla pod, 10 teaspoons Neuhaus cocoa powder,
160 gr Origine Neuhaus Sao Tomé chocolate (or West Africa or Occumare Venezuela, or the three)

1 Bring the milk, cream, vanilla pod and cocoa to the boil.
2 Stir for 3-5 minutes, without boiling.
3 Remove the vanilla pod and serve.

Hot chocolate sabayon

Ingredients, serves 2

6 egg yolks, 150 g caster sugar, 20 g cocoa fondant, 1 – 2 dl Marsala

Preparation (20')

1 Put egg yolks and sugar into an ovenproof dish and beat together until the sugar dissolves.
2 Add the cocoa fondant and the Marsala and heat in a bain-marie.
3 Beat well until a thick and frothy mixture is obtained.
4 Pour the sabayon immediately into tall heat-resistant glasses.
5 Sprinkle mini chocolate flakes onto the sabayon for decoration.

Origine Truffles

Ingredients for 70-80 truffles

480 g West Africa 72% chocolate, 320 g fresh cream, 1 pinch of Guérande salt

OPTION: *a mixture of chocolates of different origins gives excellent results:*
one-third West Africa 72%, one-third Sao Tomé 74%, and one-third Occumare Venezuela 71%

FOR THE COATING: *250 g chocolate fondant, 200 g cocoa powder*

Preparation

1 Melt the chocolate in a bowl over a pan of simmering water,
   mix with the crème fraîche and the pinch of salt.

2 Allow the preparation to cool in the fridge for at least 2 hours.

3 Form small balls in the palm of your hand or use a piping bag and then
   put them back in the fridge for a few minutes.

Coating

Placing each truffle on a fork, plunge into the chocolate mixture
and then roll it in the cocoa powder. Remove the surplus cocoa
and keep truffles in a cool place (15°-18°C).

Flavoured Truffles

Ingredients for 70-80 truffles

240 g Sao Tomé 74% chocolate, 120 g butter, 2 egg yolks, 120 g icing sugar, 5 cl Cointreau

FOR THE COATING: *200 g cocoa powder*

Preparation

1 Melt the Sao Tomé 74% chocolate in a bowl over a pan of simmering water, add the butter cut into small pieces and mix well.

2 When the butter has melted, remove the mixture in the bowl from the pan and add the egg yolks, icing sugar and finally the Cointreau.

3 Put the preparation in the fridge for at least 2 hours.

4 Form small balls in the palm of your hand or use a piping bag and then put them back in the fridge for a few minutes.

5 To complete the preparation, roll the truffles in the cocoa powder and keep them in a cool place (15°-18°C).

For an enjoyable variety of flavours, you can use shavings of milk chocolate instead of the cocoa powder. You can also use other liqueurs instead of Cointreau, for instance: Mandarine Napoléon, Cognac, or Armagnac.

Financier au chocolat
(small chocolate-flavoured almond cakes)

Ingredients, serves 8

50 g ground almonds, 1 g baking powder,
15 g cocoa paste (or chocolate made from 90% cocoa), 10 g cocoa powder,
45 g flour, 10 g dark chocolate, 135 g icing sugar, 75 g butter, 5 egg whites

Preparation

1 Melt the butter and then allow it to simmer
   until it becomes brown in colour.
2 Allow to cool.
3 Melt the cocoa paste and the chocolate.
4 Sieve the icing sugar, flour, baking powder, cocoa powder
   and ground almonds.
5 Put all the ingredients into a mixing bowl,
   adding the egg whites (unbeaten) gradually.
6 Add the brown butter last.
7 Pour the mixture into a rectangular dish
   measuring approximately 22 x 17 cm.
8 Bake at 180°C for 15 minutes.

→ In the 1920s, Neuhaus offered small 'think chocolate' calendars to serve as a reminder of the dates when a gift of chocolates should be offered. Private collection.

1920

1921

1924

1925

1926

1930

1933

1934

1935

1936

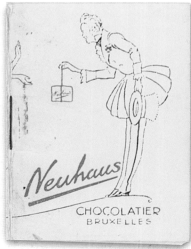

1937

1939

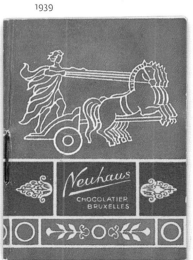

1925

1924

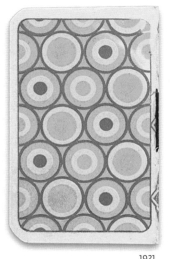

1921

1920

1934

1933

1930

1926

1939

1937

1936

1935

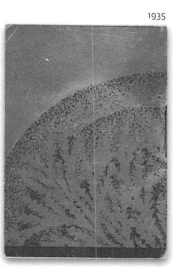

Photography

This list comprises only the data concerning the copyright or origin of the illustrations that are not accompanied by a caption.

Bridgeman Art Library: 15, 44, 58, 67, 80-81, 87, 114, 117, 121, 124, 181, 186, 187; Alinari : 123; Archives Charmet : 62 (top), 63, 70, 71, 77 (bottom), 115, 116, 126, 142, 143, 144, 145, 176; Elizabeth Banks: 77 (top); Bonhams, London: 183; Lauros-Giraudon: 64, 84, 90, 109; Roger Perrin: 79, 141; Barbara Singer: 78, 140; The Stapleton Collection: 27, 68; Whitford & Hughes, London: 180; Peter Willi: 185 – Guy David: 1, 16, 18, 24 (centre), 25, 35, 37, 38, 40-41, 42, 73, 74, 82, 102, 129, 137, 151, 156, 158, 161, 162, 163, 164, 165, 167, 168, 171, 194, 198, 202, 205, 208, 211, 213, 214, 217, 218, 220, 223, 224, 227, 228, 232 – Vincent Everarts: 22, 24 (except for the centre), 65, 66, 76, 88, 94, 95 (right), 96, 119 – Philippe Lacombe / Jean-Pierre Busson: cover photographs (front and back), 2, 12, 29, 240 – Philippe Lacombe: 235; Jorge Léon: 192 – Marchand R.: 26 – Marie-Pierre Morel: 201, 231 – Olivier Polet: 130, 132, 134, 135, 138, 146, 152, 155 – Reunion of national museums, Martine Beck-Coppola: 69, 85, 86; Jean-Gilles Berizzi: 128; Gérard Blot / Christian Jean: 106; DR: 148; Philippe Migeat: 174; François Vizzavona / Maryse El Garby: 113

© 1990. Photo Scala, Florence. Courtesy of the Ministero Beni e Att. Culturali : 89, 111; HIP: 112.
© 2006. Musée du Quai Branly, photograph by Hughes Dubois / Scala, Florence: 49
© 2007. Musée du Quai Branly / Scala, Florence: 54, 57
© 2007. Sabam Belgium: 80-81, 116, 121, 149, 186
© 2007. Sabam Belgium – H. Matisse Succession: 185

© Éditions Racine, 2007
52, rue Defacqz – B-1050 Brussels, Belgium
www.racine.be

D. 2007, 6852. 21 – Legal registration: October 2007
ISBN 978-2-87386-533-7

Published in Belgium

ICONOGRAPHY RESEARCH: Geneviève Defrance, Verlaine
LAYOUT: Steven Theunis, Armée de verre, Gentbrugge
PHOTOENGRAVING: Steurs, Antwerpen
PRINTING AND BINDING: Imprimerie Lannoo, Tielt

This work was completed and printed in Belgium on 1st October 2007

Have you succumbed to Temptation?